Beyond Recovery

A Journey of Grace, Love, and Forgiveness

Shawn Langwell

For Seth Adam Langwell
The "Wheelie King"

Table of Contents

Prologue

"He who has a why to live for can bear almost any how."
- Friedrich Nietzsche

Have you ever stopped to think about why things happen the way they do? Why does the sun rise every morning and the sun set every night? Why do some people seem to be happy most of the time while others struggle to get through each day? Why do some go with the flow while others sit on the shore waiting for a better boat? Who knows? I do know this: The longer I live, the more I feel like life is merely a series of events preparing us for the next one—a dress rehearsal; it's about practicing, taking risks, being willing to fail, and finding the strength to get back up and try again.

I have stumbled, fallen, and have experienced great joy and great heartache. I have been held captive by my own fears and made bad decisions. I have also chosen well and made good decisions. Along the way, however, I have grown to trust that everything happens for a reason, even if I don't like the outcome.

Through trial and error, mistakes and failures, taking risks, skinning my knees, having my heart broken, overcoming tragedy, experiencing great joy—and great loss; through grief, fear, anger, resentment, and even reconciliation and forgiveness; through the multitude of joys and sorrows and plethora of experiences I've played over and over in my mind like a broken record—all have, in some way, molded my view, shaped my attitude, or made me a stronger person.

The inner battles I have faced were not fought alone. Many required me to surrender my will and ego; to humble myself, leaving pride at the curb. I had to learn to ask for help and seek out the advice of others. Through that advice and practice, I developed an inner strength, a sense of faith, and reliance on God (my higher power) to guide me and carry me through every challenge. In the process, I changed. I began to look at the world through a new pair of sunglasses. I stopped focusing so much on my selfish wants and desires, and began to look to the needs of those around me. My inner battles have taught me to take my eyes off myself and put them onto others.

We all choose our own path. In the pages to follow, I will share some of the experiences, events and stories that have had an impact on my life. It is my hope that they encourage, inspire, entertain, and touch your heart. These are not necessarily unique to my journey, or, perhaps anyone's. What is unique, though, are the precise events that each of us experience, and how they may impact and affect our lives, or the lives of those around us.

Some events may bring us to our knees, begging for help. Others may melt our hearts with joy. Some may even be worthy of a story or two. While other experiences are too painful to share and remain locked away in our hearts, kept close to our chest for our entire life, never seeing the light of day. Some stories are brought to light in a dream so vivid they cry out to be told.

Chapter 1
Jump!

With wobbly knees, I stood at the edge of the three-foot diving board. I was not quite two. My heart pounded. The sun's rays filtered in through the glass canopy of the Sutro Baths that towered a hundred feet overhead. Iron arches and buttresses crossed over several salty, ocean-fed pools supporting the fragile glass panes above.

A maze of concrete walkways lined a variety of pools: some had long corkscrew slides; others were deeper with both high and low diving boards. The air was salty. I could hear adults and kids laughing and splashing as they played in the many pools of the bath house.

I felt so small as I looked over the edge. The water seemed to be a hundred feet below. My father, Jim, and some of his friends treaded water, exhorting me to jump.

"You can do it!" my dad encouraged me. "I'll catch you!" he promised, smiling.

No. It's too high. I thought, trembling.

My dad's friend nudged me along. "You can do it, jump! Your dad will catch you. On the count of three. One. Two…" I took a deep breath. "Three!" He nudged me off the edge as I leapt off the diving board. The short drop was a rush—anxiety followed by exhilaration as I splashed into the cool water between my father's loving arms.

"Yeah!" I exclaimed. "Again!"

I'd come back to that diving board many times in my mind over the years, usually when I wanted to remember what it was like to take a leap of faith.

I loved my dad. I trusted him. He worked as a fireman for the San Francisco Fire Department, and my mom took care of me. In one of the earliest photos I've seen of my father, when he was eighteen, he resembled James Dean—and a big part of him had that same rebellious spirit. He had jet black hair that he slicked back, and he was wearing jeans and a white V-neck t-shirt, with a pack of smokes rolled up in the sleeve. He was a handsome man with a wonderful smile and a huge diastema between his two front teeth.

My mom, Joan, was a pretty buxom blonde who was head-over-heels in love with my father. They were madly in love as high school sweethearts and they eloped, quickly becoming young parents—my dad, was twenty-one and Mom was nineteen.

When I was two, my brother, Kelly was born. I was curious, but I was also jealous. Before, I had had all my mom's attention. Now, I felt I had to compete for her attention with my younger brother. To keep me occupied while my mom took care of Kelly, my mom and dad got me a cat. But it ran away. So they got me another. That one ran away too. I got a third cat, a fluffy grey tabby that I named Smokey, just like the others.

One morning, Smokey woke me up. My room had a small double hung window that overlooked the back yard ten to twelve feet below. Somewhere, I had heard cats had nine lives, and was fascinated at how they always landed on their feet when they jumped off counters, ladders, whatever.

I figured I'd see if they could "always" land on their feet. I grabbed Smokey under her shoulders and dropped her out the window. "Meaooow…" she screamed—I laughed out loud as she hit the ground on all fours. Over the next few months, I'd play superman with the kitty at least five or six more times. Each time she flew through the air, she'd meow the cutest screech—"Meaooow!" At the time I thought it was hilarious. She'd almost always come back. But over time, she'd had enough. The last time she hit the ground as usual on all four paws, then leapt up on the neighbor's fence, looked back for a brief moment as if to flip me off, then took off like a bat outta hell along the top of the fence, never to be seen again.

Weeks later, my mouth watered as I awoke to the smell of bacon coming from the kitchen just off my bedroom.

I shuffled in to see what was for breakfast.

"Well, good morning sunshine!" my mom said with a big smile. "Hungry?"

"Yeah! Are we having bacon and pancakes?" I asked, with a hopeful smile.

"Yes…your favorite. Have you seen Smokey?" she asked while turning the bacon. "I haven't seen her in days."

"No…I don't know…she probably ran away," I said, looking down. I felt bad telling a half truth.

"Why would she run away?" my mom pressed.

"Um, I dunno," I mumbled, shrugging my shoulders. "Can I have scrambled eggs, too?"

"Yes, dear. Go wash up. Breakfast is almost ready."

I quickly washed my hands, then I climbed up the chair and sat on the phone book where I dug into a breakfast feast of crisp bacon, buttermilk pancakes dripping with syrup, and scrambled eggs. My little brother was quietly entertained with his oatmeal as he sat in his yellow high chair. He wore a blue bib with a little chick in the corner. Oatmeal dripped from his lips and smeared across his bib. My mom gently scooped up a spoonful, blew on it, and then opened her mouth. "Open," she said.

Kelly opened and took the spoonful and immediately opened again. She did it again, and gently scooped the overflow from the corners of his mouth.

Even though he was two, he wasn't totally adept at feeding himself yet. Either that or, like many moms, she enjoyed feeding him. It's what moms do. She'd teach him how to hold a spoon, as well. Usually she'd wait 'til he got a few spoonfuls down just to appease his hunger pangs, before letting him try it on his own.

I sat and ate my bacon and eggs while I watched.

"Here," she said wrapping his hand around the spoon. She'd scoop then guide him to eat from the spoon. "There you go. That's a good boy."

Kelly smiled.

She chuckled, "Hungry, huh?"

He nodded and smirked. She then repeated the process....
Scoop. Blow. Mouth opened wide as she continued to feed my brother.

"Mom, can you cut my pancakes?" I asked, waiting to taste the maple syrupy deliciousness.

She placed a spoonful of oatmeal in the tray of my brother's high chair. "Here try it," she said, and handing him the spoon, then turned away from him to help me.

"There you go, sweetie," she said, cutting my pancakes into bite-sized triangles. Meanwhile my brother scooped his oatmeal onto his spoon and flung it across the room. It hit me right in the face.

"Ha! Ha!" Kelly laughed.

"Mom! Kelly threw his oatmeal at me!"

"Oh Kelly, that's not nice," she said wiping it off my face.

He grinned. Even at two, he was a charming 'shit-disturber.' I went back to my pancakes and gobbled them up, getting syrup all over my hands in the process.

"Mom, I need to wash my hands…"

"Okay, sweetie. Go wash up and don't forget to brush your teeth."

She turned her attention back to my brother, and repeated the routine of scoop, blow, open, spoon, wipe—opening her own mouth, of course, just as millions of mothers have done for a long time. I washed my hands, brushed my teeth and returned to my room.

Usually after breakfast I would play with the cat, even though my eyes would get itchy from petting her. But today, there was no cat. Smokey had hit the road, so I played with my Hot Wheels instead.

My mom went to start the dishes and left my brother unattended again in his high chair—with his weapons—he had scooped another spoonful of oatmeal and flung it all the way across the room, hitting the far wall, barely missing my mom. SPLAT! I had to laugh. Kelly laughed. Even my mom had to laugh it off. The kid had range! Then, without missing a beat, he took the rest and dumped it over his head and laughed and laughed…

"Oh no!" my mom said, losing her sense of humor. "We're done!" In the end though, it was a good day.

When we were young, Kelly and I spent many weekends with Grandma and Grandpa Langwell. They both were fun loving people with good hearts, and were a positive influence on me. They never swore in front of us. Sure, they'd bicker as most couples do, but they were always so kind, and made sure that we were safe and well loved.

My grandma was actually the one who got me to use the "big boy" potty. As a young toddler, I was terrified of the toilet, thinking I'd fall in. To make it easier, my grandma and grandpa bought the most ridiculous gigantic yellow rubber duck that sat atop the toilet as a way to get me comfortable with using the adult toilet. I remember my first introduction to the yellow duck—it towered over me like Godzilla. It was so tall, I had to either use a step stool or be lifted onto it. That thing was so intimidating—it literally scared the crap out of me.

"Grandma, I'm scared. I had an accident," I said, one day ashamed at my inability to figure this pooping thing out.

"Oh, Judas Priest!" she'd exclaim in frustration. "Let's get you cleaned up," she said, while patiently wiping my bottom.

Anyway, it took a while before I overcame my fear of the big yellow potty duck. I remember the first time I did it all on my own. I was so proud, I ran into the kitchen where grandma was prepping dinner.

I tugged her apron, "Grandma! Grandma, I made biggies! Wanna see?"

"Ha Ha! Ha!" She chuckled loudly. She rinsed her hands and wiped them on her apron and followed me into the restroom.

"Good job!" She beamed. "Did you wipe and wash?"

"Yes." I said proudly.

"Good boy," she praised me with a big smile and smirk. "Now we can work on getting rid of that duck!" She chuckled, flushing the toilet.

Sometimes it's the simple things in life that can mean so much—an encouraging word; a word of praise. It was a proud moment.

Later, I discovered she didn't get rid of the duck—they needed it to torture my younger brother into potty training. He used it and hated it as much as I did, but it worked. His fear of that duck was incentive enough for him to learn how to use the "big boy" potty pretty quickly.

My brother and I loved to tease each other and many times we'd drive my poor grandma nuts when she had to watch us both over a weekend.

"Boys, go tinkle before we go," she'd announce as we were getting ready to go to dinner. In any event, my brother and I being the smart aleck kids we were, headed to the bathroom singing "tinkle, tinkle, little star." Then we'd drop our pants and take aim—a cross-fire, solid stream into the porcelain bowl. Occasionally we'd misfire and "accidentally" splash each other.

My grandma would always find out and made us clean up our mess. Occasionally we'd get under her skin a little too much and she'd have to call in my grandpa to teach us proper bathroom etiquette.

"Dagnabbit," he would protest. Then he'd give us a demonstration on how to take a proper piss without splashing pee all over the place. I'm laughing now because he took it very seriously. No doubt he got an earful or two from my grandma for missing the bowl, too!

Those early years flew by. I don't remember much. But there were a couple things that happened that would stick with me for a long time.

Chapter 2
Sex, Drugs, and Rock 'n Roll

The '60s were a period of incredible transformation, conflict and revolution. It was a decade when everything changed. I was surrounded by counterculture and all that went with it: sex, drugs and rock 'n roll. Later our family would be part of large extended family that lived communally for much of my youth. I was raised with a care and concern for our planet and people. It was a good childhood.

But not all of it was peace, love, and harmony. The United States was at war—the Vietnam conflict (that started in 1955 and would last twenty years) was now escalating rapidly through the 1960s. The media and press pushed the envelope of journalism with iconic photos, broadcasts, and stories of the war.

Television brought the war home. I remember sitting in my grandfather's lap, terrified as I witnessed brutal images of dead soldiers and napalm drops in Vietnam on the evening news. Closer to home, a different battle was going on. The battle for civil rights. Protests and demonstrations to end racial discrimination and desegregation broke out. The Watts riots in South Central Los Angeles and the freedom March on Washington D.C. catalyzed a movement to end discrimination.

Martin Luther King, Jr. was one of several outspoken leaders who led the charge for change. I was born into revolutionary times. I was surrounded by chaos from all directions—war, riots, and later, drugs.

One day, as I played in the sandy back yard of our Daly City home, I vividly recall my mother crying out, "Oh my God! Oh my God! Martin Luther King, Jr. was assassinated!"

I was too young to fully understand what was going on. My parents did their best to explain it to me. All I knew was that someone was shot, and I never fully understood why. This was a lot to take in as a young child. It scared me.

My earliest memories of that "revolution" were during "The Summer of Love" in 1967 and 1969—a massive music and love festival where over one-hundred-thousand people, most of them in their early 20s, converged on the panhandle in Golden Gate Park in San Francisco. All I can remember is topless women dancing with daisies in their hair, bare-chested guys drinking beer and smoking weed, and naked kids running around with flowers painted on their faces.

Beer, boobs, and weed were only a small part of what I would be exposed to at an early age.

Blue Smoke

A twenty-five gallon sugar barrel sat in the middle of the dank, hazy room. Empty packs of chain smoked Pall Mall Reds spilled over its edges. Just off the dark and dingy living room around a circular oak table, my father visited with his close friend, Sam who had recently come back from Vietnam. Rays of warm sunlight filtered down through the window panes of the sun room where they sat, illuminating the blue smoke from their cigarettes. I was told to stay in the living room and color. Sam sported a long red ZZ-Top like beard. He was a kind, jovial man who loved to say "far out."

I sat coloring in the living room. I looked up and saw Sam heating something in a spoon. A yellow tube sat on the table. My father grabbed it and tied it around Sam's upper arm. I wasn't sure what they were doing. Later, these memories would resurface and I would understand what was going on. That happened a lot. I witnessed more than most children probably should. My dad's friend grabbed a "shot needle"—a hypodermic syringe. He dipped the sharp tip into the "medicine" and pulled the plunger back. He slapped his inner arm, found a vein and shot up, then released the rubber band...

"Ha! Ha!" he exclaimed with a gruff laugh. "Far out!" Then Sam repeated the steps for my father. I stood there frightened...

"Dad, what's the matter? Why are you getting a shot? Are you sick?" I asked, worried for my dad.

"Go to the backroom, I'll be okay...just need a little medicine," he directed me.

"HA! HA! HA!" my dad's friend chuckled. "Medicine.... Ha! Yeah! That's good shit! But not just a little medicine, a little pain killer keeps the demons away," Sam said, leaning back in his chair.

"Demons? Medicine?" I asked, getting more worried by the minute.

"Go in the back, Shawn," my dad said firmly. "I'll get you when we're done."

Like a puppy who's told to go lie down, I did as he said. After a bit, I wandered back to the front room. "Dad! Dad! Wake up!!!"

He and his friend had nodded off at the table.

My dad slowly lifted his head—struggling to keep his eyes open....

"Oh.... Hi, Son." He said, looking at me with droopy eyes then turned to shake his friend, "Wake up, Sam!"

"Wow. Far out! That's some good shit...Ha! Ha!" Sam chuckled. He shook the last of his cigarettes out. Lit it and tossed the empty pack in the direction of the overflowing sugar barrel. It bounced off the top and landed on the floor.

My dad picked me up to sit on his knee. Staring out the window, he asked, "Hey, it's nice out. Want to go to the park?"

"Yeah! Can we go to the one with the merry go round where Grandpa takes me?"

"Sure!" he chuckled. I loved his smile, it showed his diastema between his two front teeth. I loved my dad.

I looked over at his friend. His head lay on the table and a long ash dangled from the end of his cigarette. The heat nearly burnt his cigarette stained fingers, snapping him out of his "nod."

"Whoa!...that was close.... Ha! Ha! Where you going?" Sam asked.

"To the park. Shawn wants to go on the merry-go-round."

"Far out...let's go," Sam said, slowly standing up.

We made our way down the hill to the park and arrived at the carousel. My dad lifted me up to the biggest horse. Pipe organ music, played as the merry-go-round started up. I held on as the horse rose and fell while the carousel circled. When the ride ended we wandered over to the swings. I sat in one and asked my dad to give me a push to get me started. I loved that feeling of flying—that momentary feeling of weightlessness, soaring higher and higher. And then the downward rush as the swing arced down. Then another upswing…

Lands End

A few months later, on a warm spring day, in 1969, my friend, Nick and I went with my dad and his friends on a hike above Lands End in San Francisco. As we started to hike up a narrow trail toward the ridge, my dad and his friends took a pill and a swig of beer. My dad bit one of the pills in half, and handed a piece to Nick and me. "Wash it down with this," my dad said, handing me his can of Schlitz. I didn't think anything of it. My dad and grandpa had let me have sips of beer before, I liked the taste. I took a sip then handed the can of beer to Nick. We continued along the soft trail. The sun filtered down through the branches of the tall Cypress trees in sharp rays. Birds chirped. I could smell the ocean. We hiked for a bit more then I started to feel funny—all my senses seemed heightened and time slowed down.

Soon we came upon an old concrete bunker. As we stood outside I peppered my dad and his friends with questions— "What are they? Why are they here?" I asked. My dad and his friends did their best to explain the history of the bunkers and batteries that were strategically located along the cliffs overlooking San Francisco Bay. All I remember is that they were there to protect the bay during the Spanish American

War and later during World War II. They were usually locked or welded shut. Someone had snapped the lock off this one, leaving its heavy green metal door ajar.

"Can we go inside?" I asked.

"Sure," my dad said.

"Just be careful, there might be a bomb inside," one of my dad's friends joked.

"Or, there could a bad guy inside," another quipped, as they tip-toed toward the door.

Whatever they took and gave me was starting to kick in. My head felt fuzzy. I moved back a few steps, and stood watching with white knuckles as they approached the bunker. Then one of them quickly flung the door open while another yelled, "BOOOM!" They all laughed hysterically as they fell over backwards, groaning as if attacked.

"No!" I shouted. My reaction only made them laugh harder. I felt helpless. I wanted to go home.

The white pills we took were MDA. MDA is a drug similar to MDMA or Ecstasy, but more like a cross between LSD and Methamphetamine. It can induce intense feelings, greater awareness of past, and self-insight with psychedelic-like hallucinations. My dad and his friends were just starting to peak and so were Nick and I. My legs were wobbly. I felt aware—sharply aware, but was uncomfortable because I didn't feel right. Rather than listen to Nick and me complain, they all decided to take us back to the car to let us "come down" while they continued on their quest. They left and I was stuck in the car with Nick who wailed incessantly. I cannot explain the helplessness of listening to another screaming kid who was freaking out and sitting in the car high on a hallucinogen. Eventually, I fell asleep. I have no idea how long they were gone, nor do I recall much after that.

I mention this here because years later when I found out what he'd given me when I was only five-years-old, I was pissed at my dad for a long time. Fortunately, many years later I was also able to have a conversation with my father about this, and many other things he did that hurt me. For my survival, it was necessary to muster all the courage I could to forgive him. It may seem counterintuitive to forgive someone who caused great pain or who caused mental, physical, or spiritual damage, or in this case gave me a hallucinogen. However, in order for me to move beyond some of the other pain and hurt that would later imprison me, it was necessary that I forgive him.

Chapter 3
Summer of 1969

In the summer of 1969, we left foggy Daly City for sunny San Anselmo. We found a 1940s summer home with lots of windows that sat atop a hill surrounded by oak trees on Scenic Drive. A large porch overlooked the eighty-eight steps and gravel carport below. A galley kitchen, pantry, and sole bathroom lined the back of the house. Behind the house was a sunny meadow where we planted a garden. Shortly after we moved in, my mom became pregnant. It was not expected, and it put a little strain on my parents' relationship. To make it easier to bring groceries in, my dad cut a footpath through the garden and down the backside of the hill to the back door.

I loved moving to Marin. It was sunny, had lots of trees, creeks, lakes and hills, beaches, and, unlike the city, a wide variety of houses, many with large yards.

Just down the road from our new home was the Fairfax Town and Country Club. With several swimming pools for all ages and lush lawn areas for picnics, it was one of our favorite summer hangouts.

One pool had a high dive. I'd sit at its edge, dangling my feet in the water, looking up as I watched the big kids jump, dive, and do flips, dreaming of one day being able to jump off it.

One day, as I day-dreamed by the high-dive pool, a grape popsicle dripping down my hand, my dad saw my fascination and offered to jump with me. My small sticky hands gripped the steep metal staircase and we began to climb. We reached the top and slowly inched out toward the edge of the diving board. It seemed a mile up. My legs were shaky. Almost near the end of the board, my dad scooped me up in his arms and we leapt, splashing into the cool deep pool below.

"That was a blast! Let's do it again!"

There were several more jumping and diving adventures in the years ahead. One spot we frequented, was the inkwell in Lagunitas. Nicknamed for the narrow deep pool created from the Paper Mill Creek. In the '60s and '70s, it was a popular hippie hang out.

With coolers in hand, my dad and his friends would lead us across the huge water pipe to the rocky beach where we'd sit and eat while the adults smoked weed and drank Mickey's.

Years later as a teenager, my brother, Kelly, would climb the steep rocky cliff above the ink well and swan dive from twenty feet up, into the icy water below. Too afraid of smashing my skull on the rocks, I chose to jump, not dive, from twelve feet up.

Jenny Rigby

My new school was only a short walk away. I don't remember much about first grade, except I shared a desk with Jenny Rigby. She was a cute blonde that made me blush. At seven, I was still very shy. We read Dick and Jane books. We learned addition and subtraction. Math seemed easy for me, but in my haste to finish first, I'd scribble my name and the teacher would always make a stink about it. I still have to remember to slow down.

That Christmas, I was given a blue and white cowboy outfit. I was so excited to wear it to school. I proudly walked down the hill, decked out in cowboy boots with a blue shirt, chaps, and a black cowboy hat. A belt with two toy guns sat on my hips in their holsters. Back then, you could actually bring toy guns to school and not have to worry about getting suspended, or worse—shot.

As I entered the class, I spied Jenny at our desk. My mouth dropped. She was wearing a red cowgirl outfit, complete with brown cowgirl boots, a brown hat, and toy guns at her side. She also had a lasso. It was practically the same outfit as mine. I was mortified. I had to sit next to the cutest girl in the class and it looked like we planned our outfits.

At recess I heard other kids and teachers snickering at how cute we were. As soon as school was out, I ran home as fast as I could, ripped off my cowboy outfit, and threw it on the floor.

"Honey, what's the matter? Why are you so upset?" my mom asked.

When I told my mom and dad what happened, they laughed hysterically, which didn't help.

Shabbat

Being a child of the '60s, I was exposed to a wide variety of spiritual and religious beliefs, philosophies, political views, and ways of life. Never having been to church or raised with any formal religion, I had no clear concept of faith, religion, or spirituality. That changed when Deon and John, and their daughter, Amara, lived with us for a bit.

They encouraged us to celebrate Shabbat on several Fridays at sundown. Someone read prayers and we took a piece of Matzah and drank some sweet Manischewitz wine from a brass communal goblet. I couldn't stand the dry crackers, but I loved the wine. During the Jewish Day of Atonement, Yom Kippur, we fasted and said prayers. During Hanukkah, we lit candles for the Menorah and played with a dreidel. There were times when many more families showed up. My mom's Puritan parents even showed up and loved it. What I remember is the sense of calm and unity it brought to the house.

In 1970, John, who was a self-taught astrologist, taught me about the constellations. On warm evenings, Amara, my brother, and I would sit on the front porch and look up into the starry night as John helped us navigate the millions of white dots scattered across the evening sky. For my sixth birthday, he compiled a gorgeous hand inked astrological chart that he gave me as a gift. Over the years, I have occasionally looked back at that chart searching for meaning and purpose.

Even as young as six, I wanted to understand as much as I could about why we were here and what the universe was all about. Yet, the concept of God made no sense to me—I wanted to know more. I yearned to understand more about the vastness of the heavens above. *How did we get here? How did the planets, stars, and universe form? Are there other galaxies? When did it start? When will it end? What does it all mean? Why are we here? What is our purpose?*

I looked forward to warm summer evenings star gazing with John. He taught me as much as he could that summer. My dad and Grandpa Langwell added to it in the years that followed.

Later that summer, something happened that I have only told a handful of people about. One day after my dad had let me help him paint the outside of the cast iron bathtub, I went outside to play in my fort. As I approached the fort, I stopped. I don't know why. I stood at the top of the steep hill above the carport and recall looking up through the opening in the oaks. Then it felt like I left the ground—I literally felt like I was flying through the oaks and hovering above our home. I lost all sense of past, present, or future and was just floating there in a suspended state of consciousness. I have no idea how long I was "gone." I don't know how to explain it—maybe it was flashbacks from the MDA my dad gave me at five? Maybe I had an active imagination? Maybe I was visited by some friendly grays from another planet? Who knows? All I remember was floating. The next thing I recall is my mom's voice calling me,

"Shawn!"

I stood there in awe of what I just experienced. "Over here," I replied.

"Where were you? I was calling and calling and you didn't answer me."

"I was up on the hill, but I was flying!—Mom, I was flying like a bird!"

"Oh…that's nice. Please go wash up for supper."

I know she heard me, but she didn't give it a second thought. I thought it was weird that she didn't ask me more.

Perhaps she thought I was just imagining it; it was real to me and, for some reason, it didn't freak me out; Somehow I *knew* I would be okay.

Chapter 4
Brothers

A couple weeks later, my mom went into labor. My dad quickly grabbed the peanut butter and jelly sandwiches my mom kept ready in the fridge. We piled into the VW bus and headed across the Golden Gate Bridge to Kaiser Hospital on Geary. My mom was calm, but my dad still drove like he was headed to a fire. In a way, he was. We pulled into the parking lot and parked.

"Okay kids, stay here, we'll be back in a bit," my dad said. "Here's some peanut butter and jelly sandwiches if you get hungry."

"Jim, let's go now!" my mom urged, with a grimace and tears streaming down her pale face.

"Love you, Mom," I said.

"Love you guys. Be safe," she said and then waddled across the parking lot to the Emergency Room.

"Wanna sandwich?" I asked my brother.

He smiled, his dimples showing as he exclaimed, "Yeah, I'm hungry!" He grabbed the peanut butter and jelly sandwich from my hands. He sunk his fingers into the soft Wonder Bread and plopped into the driver seat of the 1968 VW Bus. He took a huge bite that squeezed grape jelly out the sides and onto his tiny hands. The sandwich was gone in three more bites, then he grabbed the steering wheel with his sticky hands. "I want to drive!" he exclaimed with his mouth still full of sandwich.

He pushed every button and pedal—anything that looked like it would make something move.

"What's this?" he asked reaching for the key in the ignition.

"No!" I said, "that's the key that starts the car." Oops. Too much information for a four-year-old. His eyes got wide and he grinned, as he turned the key. The bus lunged forward as it would if he were a teenager learning to drive a stick. I only knew what would happen because around the same age, my grandpa had left the door to his Jeep open with the keys in the ignition. Back then, I had snuck into the driver's seat of my Grandpa Langwell's Jeep and turned the ignition. It lurched forward and scared the crap out of me. When it jerked forward, my grandpa's revolver slid out from under the seat. I reached for the leather holster.

"Em! Get that boy before he hurts himself!" my Grandma called out to my grandpa and he came running up and scolded me just as I was reaching for the gun.

"Stop it, Kelly!" I shrieked, the memory of my past still fresh as I turned the key to my father's bus and pulled it out of the ignition. "You almost got us killed!"

"Nu uh…I can drive."

"No you can't."

"Yes I can. Dad lets me drive."

"Well he lets me, too. But that's not driving, it's just steering."

"That's driving," he said with a smirk. "Like this," he jerked the steering wheel back and forth, "See? I'm driving."

It was getting warm in the car, and it seemed like my mom and dad were gone forever. Then I saw my dad approaching us from across the parking lot. He held two shiny green cans in his hands.

"Hi boys. Thirsty?" he asked, opening the two cans of ginger ale and handing one to each of us.

"Yes! Where's mom? Where's the baby?" I asked before taking a big gulp of my favorite pop.

"She's in the hospital. She's almost ready, just a bit more."

"Can we come?" I asked.

"No boys. No kids are allowed in the delivery room. But we should be out soon okay?" He said, rubbing each of us on the tops of our heads and gave us a kiss.

"Love you." My dad smiled.

"Love you, too!" We replied, disappointed that we would have to wait a little longer in the car.

As soon as he left, I looked at my brother with a grin.

"Race you," I said holding up my soda. "Mark-getset-go!"

We gulped and chugged our ginger ales until the cans were empty.

"BUUURPPPP" my brother belched loudly and laughed ginger snot out of his nose.

I laughed and burped, which made him laugh and burp again. Brotherly bonding.

Now, in the Kaiser parking lot in June of 1970, after chugging a ginger ale and burping like boys do, we both had to pee. My dad had told us to stay in the car until he got back. We couldn't wait.

"C'mon Kelly, let's go pee," I said, opening the door.

"You mean—tinkle." We laughed and then peed right there in the parking lot.

"AHHH!" I exclaimed as we pulled up our pants and climbed back into the bus.

Shortly thereafter, my dad returned with a big smile on his face.

"Guess what boys? You have a new brother, his name is Seth."

"Can we see him?" I asked.

"Yeah, let's go." he said reaching for the keys. "Where's the keys?"

"Oh…. Here," I said, sheepishly handing him the keys, "Don't ask."

He took the keys, and scooped us up into his arms, closed the door with his knee, set us down and held each of our hands as we skipped across the parking lot to see our new brother.

"This way, boys." My dad led us to an elevator. "Push three, Shawn," he said.

I started to push three but Kelly pushed every button he could reach, including three.

"I pushed three," he said with a smirk, knowing that he probably did something he shouldn't have.

"Quit it, Kelly!" I snapped.

My dad laughed, "C'mon, boys knock it off!"

Ding, second floor. Ding, third floor. The doors opened.

"This way," my dad said, leading us down a busy hall filled with nurses and doctors. The smell of alcohol filled the air. We passed a gurney. Down the hall a woman screamed.

"Is that mom?" Kelly asked, a worried look on his face.

"No. Someone else is having a baby," my dad replied.

"Then, why is she screaming?" I asked.

"It can be painful," he replied casually, not wanting to answer twenty questions. "Here—this room," he said, waving his hand.

We turned into the room. A big window ran the length of the back wall. Our mom sat upright in a big bed. Her long blonde hair fell over her shoulder. In her arms, swaddled in a warm hospital blanket, was our baby brother. She glowed and wore a big smile.

"Hi boys," she said sweetly. "Come meet your new brother."

He sat there with his eyes barely peeking out, a blue cap on his head and a red strawberry on his cheek. My dad lifted us onto the edge of my mom's bed.

"Say hi to your new brother, Seth."

"Hi Seth," I said, not sure what to do next. "Can I touch him?"

"Sure, just be gentle. Here," she took my finger and put it on Seth's tiny hand. He instinctively closed his grip, holding onto me in a delicate fist.

Kelly, seemed apprehensive, not sure if he wanted to touch him.

"Kelly, want to say hi to your new brother?" my mom asked.

"Uh—okay," he said. She then proceeded to place Kelly's hand on Seth's.

"Hi," he said, shaking Seth's hand, then turned to my dad, "Can we go? I'm hungry."

We said our goodbyes. Our mom had to stay overnight with Seth. My dad, Kelly, and I headed back across the Golden Gate Bridge to San Anselmo.

We approached the "Hub" in San Anselmo—a six way intersection with roads connecting or leading to/from San Rafael, Fairfax, San Anselmo, Ross, and Kentfield. The light turned red.

"Who wants tacos?" my dad asked.

"I do! I do!" we both exclaimed.

He took a sharp right and we parked and went into Taco Bell for our ten cent tacos.

This was one of our favorite spots, so was the Orange Julius across street or the Doggie Diner on 19th Avenue, just past San Francisco State University.

There's something special about sharing a bunch of tacos with your dad. It wasn't anything spectacular, but he often liked to stop on any road trip and get us food, snacks or treats.

He probably got that bug from his parents. They also loved to stop at places like Taco Bell, or the Smorgasbord on the way to their property in Mariposa, or big plate truck stop diners, and, of course, the "Hot-House" on Mission in Daly City.

Now as we pulled into the gravel driveway, we faced the steep climb with a belly full of tacos.

Sheila, our German Shepherd wagged her tail, hungry and happy to see us. My dad opened a can of Alpo and gave her a cup of Purina dog chow. She gulped down her dinner nearly as quick as we had inhaled our tacos.

"Boys go get ready for bed. Shawn, can you help your brother with his pajamas?" My dad asked me.

"Sure." I replied.

"I'll come tuck you in soon." he said, turning to his record collection to put an album on.

We climbed down the steep black spiral staircase to our room, which sat just off our parents' room. A small window and a glass French door faced the lower patio with a built in barbeque outside our room.

I helped my brother up the ladder to the top bunk and slipped into the covers of the lower bunk. Crickets chirped outside. The sweet aroma of ripe kumquats wafted in from the tree just off the patio.

Sheila slowly came down the steep stairs and curled up on the foot of my bed. My dad followed shortly after. His five o'clock shadow was prickly on my soft face as he hugged and kissed us good night.

"Goodnight boys—love you," he said heading back upstairs as he turned off the light.

"Goodnight Dad," we said. "Love you." Thoughts of my new brother filled my head. *What will he be like? Will he be funny? What will it be like to have two brothers?* Sheila warmed my feet and soon I was fast asleep.

The next day we returned to the hospital to bring my mom and new brother home. All I really remember is that he cried a lot and smelled like baby and baby poop.

The rest of the summer was filled with trips to the beach, fishing with my dad and Sam at China camp, and camping along the Sonoma Coast at Wrights beach with his friends.

The Land

The following summer, we made a trip up to "the land." The land was eighty acres of open redwood wilderness in Humboldt County that some friends of my dad, Ben and Shelly, co-owned. A Buckminster Fuller designed Geodesic Dome was the primary living area. It had three levels of sleeping lofts. The property was completely off the grid. It had no electricity. Water was piped in from a natural gravity spring. A wood stove served for cooking and heat in the winter. It also heated a forty gallon hot water tank. It had one large bath tub and a generator to run a 1940s wringer washer.

We parked and waited as Ben unlocked the rusty iron gate. We drove through and secured the gate behind us. The main property was set back two miles from the main road. On future trips this trek would be a muddy, messy adventure. Moms, kids, and dads would have to shimmy across felled redwoods that spanned the gorge and swollen stream forty feet below.

It was a challenge, especially in the rainy season when we had to transfer supplies across a slippery tree. Fortunately, no one ever fell. I didn't know how we made it, but we did. Once across, one or two of the men, usually Ben or Mike (who was another family friend who lived on the property year round), or my dad, would run the mile and a half up the dirt road to get the 1957 blue Chevy pick-up or the baby blue 1965 Toyota Land Cruiser so we could transport our stuff up to the dome. Some would walk ahead while others stayed back with our food and belongings. I have fond memories of our visits to the land. It was fun hanging out and being together as one big, happy, hippy commune; there were over six families with six to eight kids that would be up there at various times. I visited at least four or five times. This trip was easy though. We drove the dirt road up to the dome and settled in. Days were spent hanging out by the stream or tending to the organic garden.

At night, we'd sit around the campfire roasting marshmallows, while the adults and drank homemade beer, smoked weed and shared stories.

One night, as we were sitting around the campfire roasting marshmallows, one of my dad's flamed up. As he waved the stick and blew on it, the white-hot, gelatinous, molten, blob of sugar slid off the stick and landed on his eye, causing a serious burn. He howled and cussed. Someone ran and chipped a piece of ice off the block in the kitchen area and placed it into a cloth that my dad held over his blistered eyelid. He took a few nips off his brandy and a hit off a joint, and then he went back to roasting marshmallows with us. Later, he patched it as best as possible with gauze and adhesive tape. I don't remember much else from that trip. But it seemed like any time we went on a road trip, there was always some story or adventure or situation that would become a story to be told over and over.

When we got home, my dad went to the doctor. He was instructed to wear a blindfold for a week while the skin healed. I became his helper. My dad was an avid reader, but now he was left with little to do besides listen to music. He seemed different. I don't know if he was high on acid or what, he just seemed spacey. He asked me to pick out his favorite artists—The Beatles, Santana, Procul Harum, Bob Dylan, Otis Redding, Jefferson Starship, The Byrd's, Joe

Cocker, Jefferson Starship, The Youngbloods, etc. I spelled out the titles of each album so he could choose which ones he wanted to listen to. He picked five or six albums I then placed onto the spindle of the turntable to play.

I loved helping my dad. I just wanted to be close to him. I curled up on his lap and listened to music with him for a bit. There is something special about a relationship between a father and his son in many more ways than one. It probably is the same for a mother and her daughter. But for me, it just felt good to cuddle up on my father's chest and listen to some of the best music written over the past forty years. I still have those albums. Like us, they are scratched and well-worn.

In the fall of 1970, there was a huge thunderstorm. When it rained it sounded like buckets of water being poured out into the patio. The thunder and lightning freaked me out. I also used to have dreams of spiders and snakes and was afraid of the Boogey Man. My dad would ensure there were no monsters in the closet by making a big show of shining the flashlight and rattling the hangars, "See? It's just hangers—no Boogey Man!" Then he would tuck me in and assure me that it's all clear. I could feel his sharp whiskers as he kissed me goodnight. Sometimes he'd lay by my side, rubbing my head and protecting me until I fell asleep.

A Downhill Ride

When I was seven, my mom gave me permission to go for a bike ride on my own. It was the first time I was allowed to ride my bike down the steep hill unsupervised. I had ridden with my dad before, but this was my first time slaying steep Scenic Drive by myself.

I climbed onto my purple Schwinn with the banana seat and took off. I had to pedal up a slight hill then coast down the other side. I daydreamed I was riding a rocket ship and how cool it would be if my purple bike had jets coming out the back with flames so I could fly like Flash Gordon or an astronaut.

I coasted downhill, around the first turn, and waved to Mrs. Wagner who was at her mailbox in front of their red country house. I was so proud to be riding on my own. The hill became steeper. I picked up speed. The next corner was a little sharper. I pushed back on the pedal to hit the brakes. Nothing. I pushed again, this time harder. Still nothing.

Oh no. No brakes! My heart raced.

A white Pontiac slowly made its way up the hill. I was headed right toward it. *No problem*, I lied to myself—*I got this.* Trying not to panic, I slammed my foot down on the pedals again and again—still, no brakes! Panic set in. A brick wall and staircase were to my right, and the "Great White Shark" of a Pontiac was to my left and getting closer, fast. I looked at the wall—the car—the wall—back to the car. *I'll jump like Superman*, I thought. But that only happens in the movies. In an attempt to slow down, I dragged my feet, causing the front wheel to jog left and straight toward the approaching car.

"No brakes!" I screamed. Completely helpless and out of control—*Oh no, I'm gonna die!* I thought.

In a last ditch effort to avoid the car, I somehow turned the bike hard to the right...then BAM! I crashed face first into the moss covered brick wall! Pain shot through my face. I screamed in agony. The people in the Pontiac stopped the car immediately to help. My face was covered in blood. Wailing, I called for my parents—"Mom! Dad! Help!"

I could taste the blood in my mouth. My gasps sent a sharp pain to my gums. I had smashed one of my front teeth—so much for being a superhero, let alone, a big boy riding alone for the first time. I cried as the driver and passenger, tried to help me. The driver was a thin black man with a huge afro. The passenger was a thin white woman wearing a white leather jacket with tassels and tight white bell-bottom pants. I was so afraid. I literally thought I was going to die. All I wanted was my mom or dad to come to my rescue; to make the hurt go away…

Grandma and Grandpa Langwell

My Grandpa Emmett and my Grandma Pauline were wonderful people. They knew how to have fun, and liked to party and entertain too. At family gatherings, they'd be "in their cups", as my mom referred to it—tipsy. After they had a cocktail or two, their laughter got louder. My grandpa preferred red wine—Carlo Rossi Burgundy—be-bop as he called it, probably because it made him want to do a little jig after he took a swig.

My grandma was a great listener and story teller. She had a great sense of humor, and loved to tell jokes. Later, as a young adult, she always had a good joke for me when I called her to say hi, usually something a little naughty or off-color. With her southern upbringing, she was not shy about her "opinions."

As a child I remember sitting on my grandpa's lap after dinner. It was the late '60s, early '70s, and smoking was still popular. My grandpa would sip his red wine and enjoy an after dinner Viceroy Cigarette. Sometimes he'd even let me have a little sip of his "be-bop" while we read Dr. Seuss books or watched TV. *Mutual of Omaha's, Wild Kingdom* was one of my Grandpa's favorites. I loved Marlin Perkins' narration. He built the suspense of a hungry lion stalking its prey from the cover of tall grass, eyeing the water buffalo, followed by the chase as the water buffalo ran down the muddy embankment, narrowly escaping the sharp claws of the lion to live another day.

My grandmother would join us after cleaning up the kitchen. She'd pick her teeth with a mint-flavored Stim-U-Dent and work her crossword puzzle while watching TV.

Other nights we'd watch *Laugh-In*. I'd always crack up when Lily Tomlin would do her Ernestine phone operator routine…"One Ringy-Dingy" followed by her signature pig snort. I was far too young to get the humor, but my grandmother's laugh was so infectious, I'd laugh whenever she did, which only made her laugh harder because she knew I didn't get the joke.

On Sundays, my parents would usually show up for dinner and we all would watch the *Wonderful World of Disney* together.

My grandparents had a good life. They were good people. I never really realized how fortunate I was to spend so much time with them until they were gone. I miss them dearly.

I got to do a lot of fun, cool exciting things when I was little. There were road trips to the Grand Canyon, camping along the Sonoma coast at Wright's Beach, or fishing at Kirby Cove and later at China Camp, and trips to the San Francisco Zoo.

One of my favorite places to go was Playland at the Beach. It was near the end of its illustrious history. But like the nearby Sutro Baths, I was able to experience it for a short time before they shut it down in 1972. I especially loved the bumper cars and the fun house, but to get to them, you had to pass by Laughing Sal. She was a 6' 10" pasty faced, red headed mechanical papier-mâché character, with a sinister laugh that scared the crap out of thousands of little kids, including me.

Once safely past Laughing Sal and inside the fun house, we'd make a beeline for the huge three-story wooden slide. Kelly, my dad, and I would all slip into burlap sacks and race down the smooth varnished oak slide, while my mom watched, holding our baby brother Seth. If we were lucky, we'd catch air off one of the bumps and bounce down the rest of the way.

After the slides, we'd head to the human turntable. It was like a playground carousel, only automated without any bars to hold onto. We'd find a spot at the center of the disc. The ride would start spinning slow, then get faster and faster until one by one all the kids were flung off against the padded skirt encircling the ride. It was a blast!

Santa Venetia

In the fall of 1971, we moved again, this time to Santa Venetia. I was glad that, once again, my mom and dad had found another home that was within walking distance to school.

It didn't take me long to make a new friend, Ernesto. His parents were full blooded Italian. His mom was a knockout, with shoulder length black hair and a beautiful smile. He invited me over for dinner one night. It was the first time I had polenta. It was delicious, but I felt like I didn't belong, they were different—straight, not hippies. Everything felt so formal—from the Italian blessing before dinner, to the fine table settings, to the polite dinner conversation. His mom and dad asked me a bunch of questions about my family. I don't remember what I said, but it was definitely awkward.

Our home life was very different than Ernesto's family—we shared the house with another couple, Tim and Barbara. Barbara was pregnant and wanted to have a home delivery.

It seemed like there were always people over at our house when my dad was home. On occasion, when he and his friend, Sam had a good day fishing, he'd invite a bunch of his friends and their kids over to feast on fresh caught flounder caught at Kirby Cove or striped bass from San Pablo Bay at China Camp. The adults sat at the big table and the kids were relegated to the "kids" table. That just meant, Kelly and I and any other kids who were there could tease each other, blow bubbles in our milk, and flick peas at each other, until my dad snapped, and sent us away from the table.

One afternoon, I heard my mom and dad arguing in the downstairs bathroom. I was scared for her. I had never really heard them argue before. I don't know why they were fighting, but she was yelling and screaming, telling him to get away from her. I opened the door and saw blood coming from my mom's nose. I immediately jumped on my dad's back and threw my arms around his neck, "Leave mom alone!" I punched at his arms and tried to kick him. He pulled me off his back and calmly set me outside and closed the bathroom door. I would find out later that my dad was feeling stressed about having a third child; that they hadn't planned on having another.

I didn't worry much about my mom and dad's argument, but I was little irritated that I had to go to yet another school, my third in the past three years.

My second grade teacher, Mrs. Petropolis, was a large cheerful woman with a head of black curly hair and a loud voice. Secretly, my friend Ernesto and I called her Mrs. "Metropolis," which was so mean, especially since she was such a kind woman and a good teacher. She taught me to read story books. I was so proud when I read Johnny Appleseed on my own. I recall learning to spell M-I-S-S-I-S-S-I-P-P-I at that time, too. I repeated it over and over and over again, driving my mom and her nuts.

I also got into a lot of trouble in second grade. That's when I had my first crush on two girls—Sarah Peeler and Nancy Wigglesworth. Nancy had gorgeous long brown hair and often wore a red jumpsuit to school. I was smitten as much as a seven year old could be. So what better way to show my affection then to slowly tug her hair when we lined up to go back into class after lunch or recess? She made a stink about it and I was reprimanded, by Mrs. "Metropolis."

"Shawn, you need to treat girls with respect and be nice. Please follow the rules and line up properly."

Sarah was shorter than Nancy, with short brown hair, and had the sweetest brown eyes. In class, I would roll up little pieces of paper and flick them at Sarah to get her attention. I was conflicted—I liked them both, but didn't know how to talk to them.

In 1972, there were lots of anti-war protests and nightly news broadcasts of the increasing death rate of Viet Cong and American Soldiers in Vietnam. I was too young to understand much of that. All I remember is that I had several nightmares about the death and carnage I witnessed on TV— I can only imagine what it was like for those on the battlefield.

I do remember though, that there was some great music from that era.

Country Joe McDonald's "I feel Like I'm Fixin' to Die" was one of those catchy upbeat songs I loved to sing—even though I didn't understand what it was all about.

One day, at recess, I found myself singing it on the playground at school. Several other classmates joined in. It was our little second grade playground concert. It was an easy song to remember and we were having fun.

Well in a conservative school singing a song with lyrics that included the words, "Fuck" and "Damn," was not acceptable. The yard monitor overheard us, and asked us to stop. I protested and pleaded my case that we were just singing. The yard monitor explained why it was not appropriate at school. But still, in my mind we were just singing. She grabbed me by the arm and hauled me off the principal's office. I don't recall what happened to the other kids.

Scared about what might happen, I bit my lip and fought back the tears. At the time, I didn't think I did anything wrong. I was just singing. I thought of running. I didn't want to go. The playground cop opened the heavy blue door to the office. She explained what I'd done to the office secretary, and asked her to contact my mom, then asked me to have a seat while she went in to talk to the Principal, Mr. Peabody.

Moments later, she led me into Mr. Peabody's office and directed me to have a seat. I was angry and scared, yet still didn't feel I did anything wrong. Mr. Peabody was a large man, 6'3"with a flat top—he reminded me of Barney Rubble of the Flintstone's. I sat in a big brown chair looking at my shoes, cowering like a puppy being scolded for making a mess on the carpet as he explained why I was in trouble and how that kind of language was not permitted at school.

"We've called your mom to come pick you up," he said, as he finished reprimanding me. "Please have a seat in the lobby until she gets here."

Our house was just down the street from the school on North San Pedro Road, so my mom was there in no time. She came in the door, and the secretary immediately ushered her into Mr. Peabody's office. As I sat in the brown upholstered chair staring at the office secretary, I could hear Mr. Peabody and my mom through the thick panel door to my right.

"Mrs. Langwell, Shawn is a good student, but he's been acting up a bit in class and on the playground...is everything okay at home?" he asked. *Wrong question*—like a momma bear protecting her cubs, my mother would always stand up to defend her children. I'm sure she shot Mr. Peabody a sharp glance—you know the sharp look of disapproval that moms master over the years to get their children to comply—well here, no doubt, the school principal was going to find out what it was like to dance with my momma bear; especially at the insinuation of a more personal issue like "problems at home." Through the thick door I heard bits and pieces of their conversation.

There was a long pause, before I heard my mom continue. "Mr. Peabody, if my son is a good kid, what exactly did he do wrong?" Mr. Peabody explained that singing, "I feel like I'm Fixin' to Die" with four or five of my schoolmates was not acceptable at a public school. It was an unpatriotic anti-war song; an anthem of controversy laced with profanity.

"Mrs. Langwell, we just cannot allow that type of language at our schools."

In a curt defensive tone she responded, "Mr. Peabody, that is a very popular song. It is played on the radio all the time. He is only seven—I doubt he even fully understands its meaning."

"I understand Mrs. Langwell," he said, with a condescending tone. "Nonetheless, we cannot have kids running around singing songs with cuss words in a public school."

"Cuss words?!" she responded with that sharp inflection that says way more than any word ever could...

"Fuck"—"Damn," he clarified. "The song starts out spelling out the word fuck."

I chuckled when I heard the principal say "fuck." The secretary giggled and quickly turned away trying to hide her amusement. It sounded funny coming from Mr. Peabody's mouth. "Mrs. Langwell," he continued with a deep serious tone. "I'm going to have to suspend Shawn for one day."

"You what?!—Suspend him?!—For singing? Are you fucking kidding me?!"

Uh oh, I thought, chuckling out loud, even though it was not at all appropriate, *you just pushed momma bear too far...here come the claws.*

"Well, that's just fine!" she huffed, then quickly opened the door. Her face was red with rage.

I wiped the smirk off my face. I'd seen that look before and it was not good. I wondered, *was she mad at the principal? The school? Me? Or all of the above? Was I in big trouble?*

"I don't really give a damn!" she exclaimed as she grabbed me by the arm and led me to the door, "because we're leaving this school!" The door closed and she never looked back.

I don't remember much after that, except, I did go back to school after the one day suspension. She was furious, embarrassed, and let me know what was what, even though she had stood up for me. The rest of second and part of third grade were a blur, but I didn't get into any more trouble at that school.

Bigfoot Country

That summer we made another trip to the Land. This time Ed, Barbara and Tim joined Ben and Shelly's family and us. We spent time floating down the Van Duzen River in Bridgeville on air mattresses, and hanging out at the stream by the bridge that would flood in the winter time. There were five kids on this trip—me, Kelly, Seth, and Tia, and Danny. All of us laughed and played at the river in the day and hung out by the campfire at night.

As we sat around the fire roasting marshmallows one of the family friends, Ed, told us all about the legend of "Bigfoot." All of us kids listened intently as he described the big hairy giant who supposedly lived in the hills around the property. The guys had been drinking beer and all got up to take a leak at the edge of the woods behind the dome. Except for the glow of the campfire, the night was dark and moonless. We sat eating marshmallows by the fire, then heard a huge crash and branches snapping.

"Oh shit," Ed exclaimed. "Bigfoot!"

We all scurried up to the edge of the forest with flashlights in hand, hoping to catch a glimpse of this fabled hairy giant in the dark forest.

"Where is he?" we shrieked.

Snap. Rustling leaves. Another loud crash to our right, behind the dome.

"Oh my God! Did you hear that?!" he laughed.

We waved our flashlights toward the rustling.

"Yeah, he's so close. I can't see him. Where is it?!"

Then, we heard a loud crack that sounded like a small tree being snapped in half. It was quickly followed by the sound of heavy footsteps, and branches crackling, as something very large moved through the forest. Our hearts raced.

"It sounds like there's more than one!" he exclaimed. "Watch out kids! They're coming this way!!!"

Even with the flashlights the woods were so dark we couldn't see anything moving. Scanning the forest with our flashlights we spotted glowing eyes. "There! Behind that tree! I saw his eyes!"

Then heard a loud "BWOHAHAHAHA!!!" as shadowy figures ran toward us kids swooping us up in their arms pretending to eat us. We squealed in delight.

While Ed was busy diverting our attention to the left edge of the property, my dad and his friends had snuck around to the right and ran at us through the woods from a distance.

They got us! We loved it!

Over the years, several families had constructed their own shelters on the property. That trip, our family stayed in a red chicken coop-like building at the edge of the grassy meadow. It offered spectacular sunrise views as the sun crested the tips of 200-foot redwoods along the top of the ridge, sending long strands of its morning glory to the meadow below. It was built by a young couple who had a daughter they named Meadow. From what I remember, it was a small one room place with a bed platform, with a small pot belly stove for winter warmth, and a long sash window on the meadow side that faced east.

It was a hot summer evening. That night, I tossed and turned and couldn't stop scratching my arms, legs, face, and privates. It was frustrating. Wondering why I was tossing so much, my mom asked what was going on.

"Mom, I itch all over!"

"Me too!" Kelly said.

My mom turned the flashlight on us. "Oh no! Jim, the boys have chicken pox!" she announced, getting up.

She checked my baby brother and he had them too.

"Are we going to die?" I asked.

"No, you're not going to die. You'll just be itchy for a while."

"We'll get some lotion and baking soda tomorrow that will help." She poured some cool water from a pitcher onto two washcloths.

"Here, this will help a little for now," she said as she daubed our sores with the cool cloth.

It helped for a few seconds then the itching came back with a vengeance.

Years hence, when it's too hot to sleep and the sheets tickle my hairy arms causing me to toss and turn and scratch all night long, I am reminded of how miserable I was with chicken pox that summer.

In the morning when we awoke, I looked at Kelly, his face was covered with pimples. For the next several days we stayed isolated in that one room shack so as not to infect the other kids. My dad had gone down the hill to Bridgeville to get some baking soda and calamine lotion which helped neutralize some of the itchiness. But the days were hot, my body felt like it was on fire with flesh eating ants. It was miserable.

My mom and dad made a paste with the baking soda and put it on our sores and implored us to not scratch or we would have permanent scars. We did our best, but a few spots hurt so much that they had to be scratched. Overall we did good, I think we each only ended up with one or two noticeable pock marks. Later that week, after our sores had scabbed up, we were back to playing in the field and enjoying the rest of our trip.

Chapter 5
Valley Kids

Several months later, my parents announced we were moving again, this time to Woodacre. With my hands on my hips and jaw set, I spoke up. "Dad...Mom...I don't want to move again...I just made friends here. Don't I get a vote?"

"I'm sorry, Son," my dad tried to console me. "We've bought a house in the country with lots of property away from a busy street with lots of room to play. I think you will love it!"

Between kindergarten and second grade, I had gone to three different schools and had made a few friends, now I'd have start all over at my fourth home and fourth school. I didn't want to but, I had no choice.

We crested the edge of the road to turn down the steep driveway in our Volkswagen bus. It felt like we were going over a cliff. We bounced down the bumpy, dirt road with enough speed to get up the sharp incline on the other side. We pulled to the end and parked. The far end of the driveway was held up by a wooden retaining wall that looked to be fourteen feet down. I looked over the edge, the hillside was littered with old refrigerators, bikes, tires, and an antique stove. It reminded me of the dump, only without the stench. I could see a rusty wheel and what appeared to be an old Frigidaire from the '40s. To my right stood what looked to be our new home—a white clapboard two story home, precariously perched on a hill. It had forest green trim and beveled glass windows. Plywood covered the lower windows of the dilapidated home, making it look condemned.

"We're going to live *here?*" I blurted out. "It's a shack! It looks like it's ready to fall down!"

"Yes, this is our new home," my mom said.

"I don't want to live here!" I pouted.

"Yeah, me either," Kelly said.

"Boys," my mom interjected, "it will be fine. You will make lots of memories here and meet lots of new friends." I had heard that line the last three times we moved. This time, I didn't believe them.

"Promise we won't have to move again for a long time?" I asked.

"I promise," she said.

I trusted them and, this time, they were right, it would turn out to be one of the best decisions my mom and dad ever made. In the weeks and months and years to follow, I met new kids who would become lifelong friends. It took a while to get used to living in the country. But in hindsight, I wouldn't have wanted it any other way.

Community

We lived communally for a short period of time with four other families. This taught me the value and importance of community. We were living out the proverb, "It takes a village"—people came together to share resources, and a life of mutual respect and cooperation. It was a simple life and a good upbringing. In many ways it has shaped who I am today. Our combined families would buy food in bulk from the old co-op in Corte Madera, which saved a lot of money.

My dad and some of his friends also started a Farmers Markets at the San Geronimo Community Center. My dad and his friends also sought out ways to live off the grid—we grew our own organic food, baked our own bread, were conscientious about our resources and saved money in the process. This is not unlike the current slow-food, organic, and green movement that has grown dramatically in recent years.

Meals were a time for all to come together. Sometimes it was a big communal meal; other times everyone made a dish to share. A couple of my favorites were my dad's homemade chicken enchiladas and Joannie's Caesar salad. We shopped at the first Good Earth on Bolinas in Fairfax. At the time, it was a small store—less than two-thousand square feet. It was one of the first organic stores in Marin, that specialized in healthy organic food predominantly produced from local farms; a tradition that continues today.

Living communally and in the valley was like one big family; there were people from all walks of life: activists, social workers, and Native Americans—Grey Wolf and Running Bear—a lawyer, artists, an astrologist, an iron worker, a farmer, writer, teacher, moms, dads, a director of Parks and Recreation, a musician, a government worker, construction workers, a painter, a fireman, a nurse, and lots of kids.

Most of our community shared a collective desire to raise healthy families and teach us about our world; sharing, caring and living life with compassion, spirituality, and love. That's the culture I was raised in. It was good for a while. But I quickly grew tired of sharing my parents with everyone else. I wanted my own space—my own room—like before we all moved in together. I grew bitter, and I let my parents know how I felt.

I think my mom and dad were also tiring of so many people living under one roof; at one point, we had thirteen people sharing one main house with two bedrooms, a dome, a converted chicken shed, and another studio type structure. We had one bathroom and a small septic tank. With that many people, it was too much for the tank, so we had to dig trenches and poop in the ground at the edge of the property then cover it with lye. That got old.

New School, New Friends, New Rules

Like many kids who start a new school, I was scared because I didn't know anyone. The class structure was also different than what I was used to. At my old school we sat at desks lined in neat rows. Here we sat in a circle.

My teacher introduced me to my new classmates, then she pulled out the math book to start the lesson. When I saw the cover, my heart sank—I recognized the text from my previous school and was upset because I had already completed all the homework problems in it. I tuned out—all I could focus on was what a complete waste of time this was. After stewing for a bit, I worked up the courage to say something. I explained to my teacher that I had already done that book and pleaded for something different, but she insisted that I had to work with the rest of the class. Frustrated, I took the book home, and, by the end of the week had finished all the practice problems and handed them to the teacher with an attitude. Oh, how self-centered I was—and still am in many ways.

At recess most of the kids were playing a game I'd never played before. I stood there watching and thinking. *How do I meet these new kids?* They laughed and yelled as they raced from one end of the tanbark-covered playground to the other. The game looked like a lot of fun and I wanted to play. There was a brief pause in the game and a very tall kid with a smile from ear to ear and a thick afro came up to me.

"Hey," he said, "you're the new kid, huh?"

"Uh, yeah," I replied shyly.

"I'm Hymie. My real names James, but people call me Hymie. Wanna be my friend?"

"Uh, sure."

"Cool. What's your name?"

"Shawn."

"Shawn what?"

"Shawn Langwell."

He had the biggest smile I'd ever seen as he extended his hand. "Nice to meet you," I said as I shook his hand. Now I didn't feel so alone.

"Hey, you want to play? It's called, 'one foot off the gutter.'"

"Yeah sure…I guess…I don't know how."

"No problem, I'll teach you."

That was the beginning of a friendship that continues to this day. I would make many more friends in the following years: Antony, Joe, PJ, Al , Kira, Ray, The Berardis, the Dorwards, Dicks, Grahams, Browns, and so many more.

In the meantime, we were settled into our new home, with two or three other families, which soon grew to a few more. In short, it was cramped. My dad wanted to build a separate home for us. He had never built a home before, but it was necessary. He drew out the plans on a yellow lined notepad and figured out what he needed to do to build it. He shared his plans with Ben who suggested that we make a trip up "the land" in Humboldt that we had all visited the summer before. There we could log some of the lumber and posts to build the house my dad had sketched out.

So, that summer my mom, dad, two brothers, and I piled into our VW bus and headed north again to Bridgeville. Ben followed us in the "Jimmy"—a classic flatbed truck. His wife, Shelly, and their kids, Tia and Danny, and several others came along, too.

We drove along the Redwood Highway through Cotati, Cloverdale, and then Ukiah where we stopped for some chainsaw gear. Four hours later, we were in Bridgeville where we stopped for some food and a soda. We all piled back into our vehicles and crossed the classic arch bridge that spans the Van Duzen. We made our way up the windy road to the rusty iron gate to the two mile road for the property. It was summer, but there had been a storm earlier in the week and the road was very muddy. My dad thought he could fly through the mud but he ended up getting stuck. After putting dry and large sticks behind the wheels, we all piled into the bus to give it as much weight as possible, hoping to get enough traction to get out of the mud. My dad accelerated forward and back several times before the wheels finally caught, freeing us from the slippery mess.

At the base of the hill, the road was interrupted by a stream. It was low enough to pass and we drove the rest of the way up to the dome and settled in, made dinner and had a good night's sleep.

The next day, my dad, Ben, and his friend, Mike, scouted the forest for the straightest trees they could find for the posts of our new home. The plan was to find seven Douglas Fir trees, cut them down, bring them back to Woodacre, then skin the bark, treat them with wood preservative, and set them in fifty-five gallon drums filled with concrete. These would serve as the primary support for our hexagonal home. Ben led the tree-cutting project. He carefully surveyed the trees looking for the straightest ones he could find and whether they would have a clean landing with minimal damage to the remaining trees. While they scouted the forest, my brothers, Danny, and I played tag.

After a half hour or so, they identified the six trees to be cut. My dad marked each with a red dot of spray paint. Ben grabbed the chainsaw and pulled hard on the nylon starter rope. The chainsaw huffed and puffed a couple times like a horse after a good run. After a few pulls it finally started. The motor echoed loudly through the soft forest. Puffs of blue-grey smoke wafted through the morning air as he revved the engine.

Ben approached the first tree. We were still playing tag, oblivious of the impending danger.

"Jim, Mike, get those boys outta the way!" Ben yelled over the rumble of the chainsaw. "Get them back here," Ben shouted, nodding in the direction of the road behind him.

"Boys! Get out the way! Come here!" My dad hollered at us, pointing to a safe spot on the dirt road.

We watched from the road as Ben revved the engine and cut a small notch on the back side of the tree in the direction he wanted it to fall. The earthy aroma of the damp forest and fresh cut wood smelled good. Ben lined up the sixteen inch blade behind the notch he'd just made and cut through. The tree was small, so a few seconds later, the tree started to fall. He yelled, "Timber!" as the tree snapped and fell with a thud on the forest floor.

We watched as he felled six more, yelling, "Timber" as each one fell. When he was done all the men started to trim the branches and load the trees onto the flatbed. Danny, my brothers and I went back to the meadow to play fetch with Danny's dog, Schlemmie. We took turns throwing rocks as far as we could and Schlemmie always came back with the one we'd thrown. She also loved to chew rocks, so much so, that she had worn her teeth down to nubs. We played fetch with her for a bit longer, had dinner, then my brothers and I went to bed.

We returned to begin building the house a few days later.

Our "Dome"

The house my dad had designed wasn't really a dome, we just called it that. It was hexagonal, with a large center post from one of the fir trees we had cut down from the Humboldt property weeks earlier. The logs needed to be skinned and treated. Earlier, my dad had hung a rope swing from a 100-year-old oak at the top of the hill above where the dome was being built. While my dad and his friends prepared the trees to become the posts; they skinned the logs with machetes, then soaked them in a wood preservative. My brothers and I played on the swing as they worked below. One of his friends, who was wasted, jumped to slap my foot, but slipped and grabbed my foot to catch his balance, pulling me off the swing and sending me flying toward that machete.

Oh no, I'm gonna die! I thought as I flew through the air. I landed with a thud that knocked the wind out of me. My dad scolded his friend, "Leave the kids alone or they could get really hurt!" I regained my breath, and went right back to swinging.

After the posts had been prepped and cured he set seven of them in fifty-five gallon drums filled with concrete. Over the next several weeks, he set joists, added a five foot walkway made of 2"x12" redwood and used 2"x6" for tongue and groove fir for the flooring. For the windows, he used reclaimed sash windows. He also built a loft for Kelly and me to sleep on; Seth would sleep on a small bed near my mom and dad's bed. The main story was complete. All that remained was a small section of floor for the second story, about twelve feet up, that would temporarily serve as the roof since winter was approaching fast. As he finished the upper level, he let Seth and me help him. Seth and I took turns handing him boards to measure and cut, then nail in place. As we helped him, it reminded me of when Grandpa Langwell let me help him roll our asphalt for the roof of their cabin in Mariposa. It was pretty high up and I was a little nervous, but I thought it was cool to be on the roof with my gramps. He was very careful to not let me get too close to the edge of the roof.

Unlike me, Seth had no fear of heights. He walked around the roof, handing my dad the biggest boards his little four-year-old arms could carry. We were almost done. All that remained was a small six-foot section near the center support pole. I handed my dad a board to cut. Then, out of the corner of my eye, I saw Seth go toward the hole. It was too late. He fell through the opening smashing his head against the edge of a steam trunk dresser below and began shrieking.

"Oh my God! Oh my God!" my dad screamed. In two seconds, he was down the opening to see how bad my brother was hurt. I never saw my dad move so quick. A small gash bled above Seth's right eye where a huge knot had already formed.

My dad cradled his left arm under my brother's neck and picked him up. He carried him up the hill and off to the hospital. I'm sure he felt terrible, but my mom was worried and pissed—"How could you let a small child on a roof?! He's only a baby!" she scolded my dad.

"We were lucky. He's okay," my dad assured her.

Seth was fine. The worst he got was a huge bump on his head. We were all lucky he didn't break his neck!

White Christmas

December 25, 1975—We awoke to a blanket of snow outside my grandparents cabin in Mariposa. It was magical— our first white Christmas. It had snowed like crazy in the middle of the night. The branches of towering Ponderosa Pines that lined their property were sagged under the weight of the snow. The five ton granite boulder that sat outside the dining room window, looked like part of a gigantic snowman.

A blanket of virgin white snow surrounded the ground and patio outside the cabin. Untouched—it was calling our name. The gifts would have to wait.

My brothers, two cousins and I couldn't wait to make tracks and have a snowball fight.

After we pelted each other a few times with snowballs, my Grandma Pauline beckoned us inside to breakfast and then to open gifts. We inhaled our bacon and eggs and pancakes and took turns shredding open our gifts. All the boys got Pogo sticks and my cousin Sheila got a bike.

"Let's make a snowman!" Aunt Bonnie suggested to my mom.

Bonnie and my mom went outside and started forming the balls for a snowman. My brothers, cousins and I followed. Uncle Pat, Dad, and Grandpa stood on the patio having a smoke while they watched.

Kelly started to make a snowman, but thought it would be better to chuck a big snowball at Seth—"Snowball fight!" Kelly cried out as he pummeled Seth in the back.

We laughed and giggled chucking snowballs at each other. My cousins, Michael and Sheila, joined in, while my mom and aunt finished their snowman. They had already made arms with branches and put a carrot in the middle of the head for a nose.

"Hey, want some coal?" my grandpa asked as he handed them two lumps of coal—he had disappeared a few minutes earlier get some from the big sack that sat near the pot belly stove used to heat the upstairs bedroom area.

"Now all we need is a corn cob pipe," Aunt Bonnie said. "Here…give him a smoke," my grandpa said, handing her a

Viceroy cigarette. It would be another five years before he quit. Michael, Seth, Kelly and I got tired of snowball fights and went in to get our pogo sticks.

We started on the patio.

"Keep an eye on those kids, Em!" My grandma shouted to my grandpa from the kitchen as she finished cleaning up after breakfast.

Kelly decided to bounce off the patio, onto the frozen ground. Before long he was hopping his way up the driveway. Seth, Michael and I followed. We hopped over rock and logs. Kelly even hopped over the frozen fire pit. It was so much fun.

There were many good times at that cabin over the years, but as a kid, that truly was the best Christmas ever.

When we got home, those pogo sticks became our favorite toy. We hopped all over our property in Woodacre—down steep hills, up the stairs—nothing was off limits. We hopped where ever we could. We even hopped over the dog! Sometimes the bottom would get stuck if we hopped into soft dirt, but we'd just pull it out and keep on hoppin'.

We played outside and had a lot of fun when we were kids—Atari Video games had not yet come out, neither had Nintendo. We lived on 3/4 of an acre and had lots of friends nearby. My friends, my brothers, and I played hide and seek, kick the can, and tag or huge games of capture the flag. We went for hikes to places like the "Hobbit Forest," and the swimming hole at the top of the ridge in Woodacre. In the summer when the grass was tall and dry, some of us would cardboard slide down the hill off Fire Road or Hill Avenue. We would catch blue gill at the San Geronimo Golf Course duck pond, or crawdads at the creek in Woodacre with nothing but a chunk of salami tied to a stick for bait. I'd play tennis ball baseball with the Giacominis and Browns after school. We built forts from redwood bark and would tumble through the soft forest floor beneath the redwoods. Life was good—simple, and fun.

The next year, my brothers and I all got Big Wheels for Christmas—one of the best toys ever. They had hard plastic wheels and were perfect for bombing down the steep road we lived on and spinning three hundred sixty degrees on a blind corner at the bottom of the hill.

Our neighbors had a son, Justo, who was around the same age as Kelly. Even though his dad probably didn't like it, we made a race track on part of their property complete with ramps and jumps at the base of a steep hill.

One year, we had kids from "The City" come to visit our school. Their eyes were as wide as saucers when we showed them how to catch lizards. There was a small hill behind the school with a large oak tree at the top. Halfway up were several large rocks covered with lichen. It was a favorite spot for lizards to warm their cold-blooded bodies. My friend, Jamie, was a pro at catching lizards. We brought a couple of the "city kids" up to the rock and made a couple of homemade nooses from the longest strands of tall "wheat" grass we could find. Quietly, we approached one of the big rocks where two blue bellies were sunning themselves. We carefully slipped the grass noose over their necks. "Got 'em!" Jamie exclaimed. We undid the noose and let the city kids take turns holding it. These kids had never been in the country before. Catching lizards was about the coolest thing they'd ever done.

In the summer, my friends and I played Marco Polo at the Woodacre Improvement Club and practiced our flipping and diving skills off the springboard.

In sixth and seventh grade, we got to go on several field trips and camping trips. One was at the Hyatt on the Embarcadero. I don't remember why we were there, but I do remember that they had a huge fountain in the lobby and people would make a wish and toss coins in it. One of my classmates saw that a janitor had left a long handled push broom resting against the wall. Without hesitation, he walked over and grabbed it, and then took off his shoes, rolled up his pants, and started sweeping up the coins in the fountain. We all scrambled to the fountain, grabbing handfuls of change. When our teacher saw what we'd done she was pissed. Yeah, it was totally wrong, but at the time it was hilarious.

In sixth grade, we got to go to Hendy Woods as a class. We spent a whole week, swimming and jumping off the rocks into the deep pool below the bridge.

Then, for seventh grade we got to camp at Yosemite in May. We camped near a stream that runs through the valley opposite the meadow under the pines.

The next day was mine and James' 11th birthday, having been born on the same day. It had been a fairly warm day, and James' idea of a birthday celebration was to dare me to jump into the frigid waters of the stream near our campsite.

We stood on the railing of a small foot bridge. He jumped first, his lips turning blue as he swam back to shore.

I stood on the rails and said, "No way, that looks way too cold."

"C'mon. It's not cold, it's all in your head," he told me.

I took his dare and jumped. As soon as I hit the water my arms and legs could barely move as I frantically tried to swim to the shore. He lied, it was like ice water.

In December, there is an annual arts and crafts faire at the San Geronimo Valley Community Center. There was always a big urn of mulled wine. That winter, James and I decided we'd have a few glasses and then "borrow" my mom's car. I snuck the keys out of her purse and went to her car. We had no idea what we were doing, but we managed to back it up without smashing another car. We pulled out of the parking lot, turned onto busy Sir Francis Drake Blvd., and then drove up to the San Geronimo School. I could barely reach the pedals, but we made it. When we got up there, James took a turn behind the wheel.

He was hooting and hollering as we circled the parking lot laughing our asses off, until his mom and mine came running up from the road, yelling and screaming at us to stop; one of our friends had ratted us out, which possibly saved us from crashing. I never did that again, but it wasn't the first time I went for a "joy" ride.

Two years earlier, my friend Joe, and I stole his mom's van in Fairfax and went for a spin around the corner. Neither one of us could reach the pedals without standing up. We pulled away from the curb and turned up a narrow road near his mom's house. Fear set in really quick as we saw a car approaching. We decided to turn around and head back. As he attempted a three point turnaround on a one lane road, he accidentally stepped on the gas too hard. The back wheels smashed against the curb, snapping the axle. Somehow, we managed to drive it back around the block. But when his mom, Susan and "Aunt" Mary came home, there was hell to pay. Susan let us know how pissed she was, but she cared deeply for us and didn't want us to get hurt.

The next few years were relatively uneventful in our new home. My dad finished the dome and it was nice to have our own space. With so many people around, and so much going on, most of my memories around this time are like tattered pictures—pieces of scenes and events and memories, most of them good. I rode big wheels and played hide and seek on the property with friends, it was just a normal childhood with lots of extra people.

Though my dad was never into sports, several of the men and friends of our extended family were—especially, baseball and football. In the winters, many of my dad's friends would come over to our house and play original Strat-O-Matic football. Several of them took it very seriously and created elaborate, hand-painted playing fields from plywood to use as game boards. They had drilled small holes in the board and used paper clips for yard chains. They used dice and players cards for simulated game play; it was the original fantasy sports game. They'd play for hours and smoke weed, drink beer and a few times even smoked heroin off foil in our kitchen. That didn't go over too well with my mom.

Kelly and I were always interested in listening to them banter and trash talk as they played and smoked out. Occasionally they'd let us have a hit off a joint and a sip of Mickey's. One time, though, Kelly was being a little too obnoxious around their game and my dad tied him by the ankles and wrists between the open studs of the wall between the kitchen and dining room to reprimand him. At first it seemed like a joke; Kelly didn't seem to mind it. But after a while, the ropes started to hurt and he wanted down. My dad ignored him. My mom found out and laid into my dad.

Over the next few months, my dad continued to expand our circle of friends, even though we already had thirteen people living with us. We started hanging out with another family acquaintance, Jerry. He was dating a young woman, Chris, who lived in an apartment in Fairfax with her two daughters, Lynne and Lori, by a previous marriage. Lynne and Lori were around the same age as Kelly and me. Our family would go over there on occasion to swim and barbeque. It was nice to have access to a pool, but besides that, my brothers and I were usually bored.

One day, after school, I came home to my mom and dad in a loud argument. Standing in the doorway, I was shocked. Rarely, if ever, had I seen them yelling at each other.

"I can't handle all three boys," my dad said, standing with his jaw set. "I never wanted to have a third. You told me you had birth control—now, you want to go to school..."

With a look of certainty, my mom stood her ground. "I never got to get a college education, and I want to be a nurse. We can manage."

"I need you to be home with the kids," my dad said, unyielding.

"I don't understand, it's what I want to do, " she pleaded, wiping the tears from her eyes. But his mind was made up. My mom left the room in a huff.

Shortly after that argument, my dad took off on a fishing trip with his friend, Terry. When he didn't come home the following night as planned, my mom appeared beside herself with worry. She tried to keep it to herself, but clearly she was upset.

The next day, as I played in the front yard, my dad pulled up. My heart sank—the bus was all scraped up and covered in red. I thought he was seriously hurt. When I saw him stagger out of the bus, I ran down the steps and wrapped my arms around him. I later found out that he and Terry had gotten really drunk and rolled the bus. When it rolled, a can of red paint that was in the back popped open and spilled all over, making the bus look like a murder scene.

To get away from my cramped house and the stresses it was causing on my parents, I started spending more time with my friend, Joe. He lived alone with his mom, and it was quieter at his house—plus, we got to see lots of movies. We loved the *Pink Panther* movies, especially the character we called "Nickel Nose." We got to see *Jaws* and later, *The Exorcist*. I had seen it once with my dad, along with a bunch of other movies that, as a kid, I probably shouldn't have seen, like *Rosemary's Baby*, *A Clockwork Orange*, *Deer Hunter*, and *Apocalypse Now*. Joe had also seen *The Exorcist* once, and we had a great idea for a prank as we sat on the edge of the upper balcony of the original Rafael theater. We waited for that infamous scene where Linda Blair is being exorcised of her demons. At the right time, we leaned over the railing and, as Linda Blair spewed vomit on the big screen, we each dumped a baggie full of tapioca pudding and watched in slow motion as it splattered on some poor bald guy's head below.

He cussed, and being the pre-teen punks we were at the time, we laughed hysterically and raced out of that theater like our pants were on fire.

Sorry dude.

Chapter 6
How Could You?

"Goddammit Jim!" my mom shouted from the terrace outside my bedroom.

I sat up with a start and went outside to see what she was yelling about.

"Where's Dad going?" I asked.

"He's leaving us!" she replied, tears streaming down her face.

"What?! What do you mean? Why? When's he coming back?" I asked in rapid fire as my dad jumped in his 1972 Blue VW bus and slammed the door without looking back.

"He's not coming home," she said as she wiped the tears from her cheeks.

"What do you mean 'He's not coming home'?! He didn't even say goodbye! Where's he going?"

"To live with another woman," she said, tight-lipped, fighting back the pain and rage.

"Who? What? You mean he's leaving us for good? Will we ever see him again?"

I was in shock. I had no idea he was unhappy. It caught me by complete surprise. Sure they had argued a bit over the years, but nothing major, mostly just married bickering. The only big fights I remember were when they found out my mom was pregnant with Seth, and when my mom wanted to go to nursing school. Other than that, they seemed happy. Now, out of the blue he was leaving us.

I stood there in shock. The man I had looked up to all my life was leaving me without saying goodbye. I cried out and started to run toward the bus, "Dad! Wait!"

Ignoring me, my dad started the VW bus and revved the engine. By now my brothers were standing there in shock.

"What's going on?" Seth asked.

"Dad's leaving and he's not coming back." I said.

Clutching my mom's leg, he hid his tears and cried out, "Dad, don't go!"

"Oh boys, come here."

Kelly stood there with an empty gaze, "Mom, what are we going to do?" he asked.

She extended her arm and held him as he fought back the tears.

"Oh, babies—come here," she wrapped Kelly and Seth into her arms, weeping.

My dad didn't even look up. With his head over his shoulder, he spun out as he backed down the gravel driveway. The muscles on my skinny neck flared with the rage I felt inside.

"Fuck you!" I screamed. "How dare you leave without saying goodbye! You fucking chicken shit!"

As he sped away, I grabbed a stinky apple juice jar filled with pee (my brothers had used it as a piss bottle since we didn't have a downstairs bathroom) and threw it as hard as I could at the bus and missed. He was already headed down the steep driveway. All that remained were a broken hearted mother, three young boys abandoned by their father, and shards of piss stained glass on the gravel drive.

"I hate you! I hate you!" I screamed as tears streamed down my face. In that moment, somewhere around April of 1978, my world seemed to collapse—the happy train came off the rails—my dad had left without saying goodbye—*What man would do that to his kids? Why? Did we do something wrong?*

"I'm so, so sorry," my mom kept saying to us. Why she apologized, I never understood. He was the one leaving us. Why should she be sorry? Maybe that's what moms do—carry the weight of the family on their shoulders. It was a sad day. Kelly seemed more pissed than sad. Seth was bewildered. My mom was a wreck. I was numb—sad, pissed, and just wanted it all to go away like a bad dream. But it was real—he was gone and wasn't coming back.

"What are we going to do?" I asked, feeling the fear set in. I never knew my mom to work. *How would we survive?*

"Mom are we going to be taken away?"

"No, boys—we'll get by. We'll survive," she assured us as best she could through the tears and pain.

That night I slept curled up next to my mom as we cried our eyes out.

In the weeks and months ahead, I agonized over what my friends would think. I was ashamed that I was another statistic, a kid from one more failed marriage, one more family torn apart.

Divorce has affected millions of kids from my generation; the "free love" and drug filled era of the '60s, '70s, and even '80s took its toll on countless children.

According to a 2011 report by the census bureau, the divorce rate rose steadily during this period.

- 1970: 33%
- 1975: 48%
- 1980: 52%
- 1985: 50%

* Information from www.census.gov.

The 2011 report also provides revealing statistics regarding children and divorce:

- 75% of children who were divorced lived with their mothers
- 28% of children living with a divorced parent lived in a household with income below the poverty line

Our family was included in these stats.

Things were scary. My mom had to find work fast. One of my mom's favorite lines in reference to her being a single mom was that she had to wear the pants and the skirt in the family. That's true. However, I naturally fell into a role of surrogate parent and took on a lot of additional responsibility as the oldest child—cooking and cleaning as well as caring for Seth.

We always had enough, but for a very brief period after my dad left, things were tight. Immediately after the divorce, we had to accept General Assistance (Welfare), now called EBT, while my mom looked for a job. We didn't want anyone to know we were on welfare, but that was kind of hard when we had to buy food with those plain white or yellow labels, and packages stamped with big black letters that read: MEAT or MILK—USDA. Those labels were like billboards saying, *you are poor.* It barely qualified as food; the milk was powdered and the meat was canned Government Issue rations. We tried to make a meatloaf out of the canned meat, but it smelled like dog food and tasted nasty. That night, we ate cereal for dinner instead. I felt bad for my mom. Despite living in extreme poverty for a couple years, she found work, and we always had food on the table and a roof over our head.

My mom found work quickly, but money was tight, especially when it came to buying new shoes and clothes for growing boys. With my dad gone, my mom couldn't afford the $50 shoes I wanted. She said that she would give each of us $20 toward shoes, but told me if I really wanted the $50 pair, I had to get a job to pay for the difference. So I did.

At thirteen, I was hired to shag balls from the driving range and to wash the carts at the San Geronimo Golf Course. Basically, I was a moving target for golfers. I'd drive out into the middle of the driving range in a cart without a protective cage, while golfers teed off from the hill above the back nine. I hated it, and I only lasted two weeks. I found another job immediately as a dishwasher for a local café. It was a grueling job, but it became the first step toward a restaurant career that would ultimately enable me to pay my way through school, buy a house, and raise a family.

My dad leaving was one of those nightmare scenes that I played over and over in my mind like a broken record. I kept wishing that he'd come back. He never did. My anger and resentment kept escalating.

I would be graduating eighth grade soon and starting high school in the fall, and he wouldn't be there. I was already going through hormonal changes and experiencing a bundle of confused feelings. I didn't want to deal with any of them, so I turned to pot.

That summer, I got stoned virtually every day. My friend Christophe and I would sit up for hours playing the game of Life. Every time one of us got married or had a kid, we celebrated by smoking a joint. I made sure to buy all the insurance for everything, probably because I didn't want to lose anything more. The rest of my summer was spent swimming and playing basketball and getting stoned.

It would be months before we actually spent time with my dad. I kept waiting for him to call. Finally he did.

Make Lemonade From Lemons

My brothers and I had to learn to adapt, to deal with the fact that our father had fallen in love with another woman, Chris. She had two daughters of her own, from a previous marriage, Lynne and Lori, who were around the same age as me and Kelly. Later, my half-brother, Tyler, was born. The first time we got to spend time with our dad after the split was very awkward. We didn't really know Lynne and Lori that well, nor had we met Tyler. Around July or August, we spent the weekend at their apartment on Sir Francis Drake near College of Marin in Kentfield.

My dad and Chris took off somewhere, leaving us alone to watch over our baby brother. It was a hot summer day, and there was little food in the house. We wanted to get sodas and something to munch on, but had no money. So we decided to set up a lemonade stand on busy Sir Francis Drake Boulevard. Shortly after we set up, a black town car pulled up. I don't know who was in it, but I like to think it was some famous celebrity. It was like a Grey Poupon commercial; the driver parked and got out of the car wearing a tux, handed us $20, and said he wanted all the lemonade. He took the pitcher and cups, handed it to the mystery person in the back of the town car. After he pulled away, we jumped in excitement. We were rich!

There would be other sporadic visits over the next several years as they moved to Rockaway Beach, the Russian River, and eventually Monte Rio.

A couple summers later, Aunt Bonnie rented a cabin on the Russian River for a "family reunion." Grandma and Grandpa Langwell stayed with her, Uncle Pat, and my two cousins. Talk about awkward—it was the first time we all had been together since my dad left.

The air was thick with contempt. Body language and looks said far more than any words ever could. My mom and grandma shot daggers from their eyes at my dad's new wife, Chris.

None of it seemed fair. But we did our best to be civil and move on.

Chapter 7
Mom Needs a Break

There isn't a playbook for parenting. In a traditional family, there are roles, but no hard and fast rules. Parenting styles typically follow tradition, whether we like it or not. Regardless, one thing is certain—we're all born into a world completely dependent upon another—usually our mother— for survival. We come in without cynicism, anger, hurt, or pain. We're innocent, unfettered by the world and the experiences yet to be. Pure. Innocent. Joyful. There's nothing in this world that compares to the love shared between a mother and her newborn child. Moms are there to nurture— to provide comfort and assure us that everything will be okay. My mother was no different; she always encouraged my brothers and me to follow our hearts. She gave us moral boundaries, but let us skin our knees, too. From the first days of school to graduation, our mother was always there. Even in the tough times when we had very little money, we always had a roof over our head, food in our bellies, and clothes on our backs. For that I am grateful. Though family dynamics vary, dads play an important role in the life of a child. They are there to teach and provide security. Often they are the parent kids have fun and play with, and are typically there to provide an element of discipline. Both parents are important in setting the values and establishing the rules for the home.

In past eras, fathers were the primary bread winners. Over the years that has changed with more and more women pursuing careers and both parents working. When one parent leaves, the family dynamic changes. Shortly after my dad left, my mom needed a break.

She let Kelly, Seth, and me know that we were going to spend a month of our summer in Humboldt County living with Ben and Shelly and their two kids, Tia and Danny.

"Mom, do we have to go? We're going to be bored out of our minds," I whined.

"You have to go. I need some time to not be a mom." I didn't ask why. It didn't matter. When my mom had her mind made up, there was no changing it.

The day came and she drove us to the Oakland Greyhound Station. The station was dank and depressing. It reeked of urine. A skid mark of diesel soot stained the outside rear of the busses.

I didn't fully understand why we had to be gone for so long. But it didn't matter now. The driver, was a spry elderly black man with a smile from ear to ear. "Where you boys headed to?" He asked, making us feel welcome as he grabbed our bags and stowed them in the luggage compartment under the bus.

"Eureka." I said.

"Good spot. Lots of redwood trees along the way." He turned to my mom.

"Tickets?" the driver asked.

My mom handed him our tickets.

"I'll miss you, boys. I love you."

"I love you, too!" we said, as she hugged us and said goodbye.

"Bye, Mom." I said.

"Be safe. Mind Ben and Shelly, and watch over your brothers."

"We'll be fine. Goodbye."

We climbed on board and found seats near the back of the bus next to the restroom.

It wasn't long before I would realize that was a mistake. At every sharp turn the waste tank sloshed. The stench leaking out from under the door was enough to make you hurl.

"That smells gross!" Seth said, not even trying to be quiet about it.

"Smells like ass!" Kelly added

A young couple a few rows up chuckled.

Ten or so hours later, we were in Eureka. The air was thick with fog and the sour smell of nearby Pulp mills. Ben and Shelly met us and drove us back to their home in Fortuna.

Two days later we loaded the car and headed up towards Bridgeville along the Van Duzen River, to spend a few days at "The Land."

In the winter, the Van Duzen was a raging river. Bridgeville is a tiny town with a population of forty-eight or so. It has a post office, grocery store, gas station, auto shop, and a school. The store sat at the edge of the river fifty feet above. A long steel bridge spanned the Van Duzen connecting Bridgeville to on the other side.

After winding our way up the hill from Fortuna, we pulled into Grizzly Creek Redwoods State Park to have lunch. Shelly had made us sandwiches. We found a picnic table and ate. The park butts up against the Van Duzen. In summers past, the river was tame enough to float down on air mattresses. Even though it was now mid-June, the river was swollen with icy water from the snow melt.

After lunch, we all walked along the soft redwood forest floor. I loved how cool and calm the redwood forest felt. The roar of the river was not too far off, raging onward over ten- and twenty-foot boulders worn smooth from centuries of storms.

In April, the area had been hit by a huge storm that flooded the campground floor creating small creeks leading to the Van Duzen when the waters subsided. The earth was light and fluffy. A few patches were exceptionally loose. It was a perfect playground for a bunch of kids. Kelly had walked ahead of us and was knocking huge chunks of loose earth off where the drainage creeks had formed on the campground floor. He laughed as one chunk he broke off made a huge splash.

Seth, Danny, Tia, and I caught up to Kelly. We raced along the forest floor trying to outdo each other, each of us screaming, "avalanche!" as we all broke off pieces with our feet. I slipped on my second one and fell on my butt. Covered in mud, I stood and raced on to the next. Kelly and Danny were already at the edge of another. Seth and I raced to catch up. The ruts in the forest floor were getting deeper as they approached the river's edge.

"One. Two. Three!" we counted off before we jumped and landed on the loamy edge of the forest floor. The water-soaked, area was already eroding, and a large chunk cascaded eight feet down the embankment, from our blow.

We quickly spied another. Seth had spotted it first and was nearly there. This one was massive. It was a dark, earthen cove near the river's edge. The rest of us had caught up.

"Seth, stop!" Ben called out from sixty feet away.

We were too busy laughing to completely hear him. A huge crack had already formed six feet back from the raging torrent. Seth had spotted the weak spot and prepared to jump.

"Shawn! Stop Seth!" Ben screamed as he raced to catch Seth.

I spun in the direction of his voice. Seth didn't, as he was determined to upstage his older brothers.

Seeing the impending disaster, Ben sprinted through the redwoods, "Seth! No!"

I started toward my brother. Ben knew the power of the raging water. We didn't; we were kids.

Before I could realize what was happening, Seth finally turned toward Ben. His right foot slipped into the water. My heart raced.

Just then, with one hand on a small redwood sapling, Ben reached for my brother, grabbing him by the shirt. He flung him away from raging waters of the Van Duzen. Seth safely landed on his butt about eight feet from the river's edge.

"Ha! Gotcha!" Ben exclaimed. As an iron worker for high rises in San Francisco, he was fearless.

As he stepped back, a six-foot wide, twenty-foot long chunk of earth was ripped away downstream, it could've been my brother.

"That was a close one!" Ben chuckled nervously. "That river has no mercy. It will eat you for lunch!" Shocked by how close we had come to losing my brother, we all steered clear of the river's edge and headed back to the car.

Chapter 8
Single Mom with Teens

Those first couple years after my dad left were a challenge for my brothers and me, as well as my mom. We all had to adapt. She had to find work. We had to step up around the house. We also had to deal with the emotional wreckage of my dad leaving us.

Being single for the first time in many years, and in her early thirties, my mom did what many do after becoming recently divorced or separated—she tried to relive her 20s by partying and dancing until late.

I was oblivious to it until she came home drunk one night. She could barely walk up the stairs. I had never seen my mom wasted like that before and it scared me. I confronted her, letting her know how much I hated to see her drunk. Inside, I felt like she didn't care and I was worried my brothers and I were going to lose our mom, too. It pissed me off, but fortunately for all of us, it was a relatively short phase.

Later, there were a few men who expressed interest in her. I recall one occasion where a burly guy showed up wasted, wanting to see my mom. I was protective of her and didn't like that a drunk guy showed up unannounced. I was not shy about letting her know how I felt.

My mom had two boyfriends over the next few years— Greg and Pat.

Greg was a carpenter who also played the conga drums, which he left at our house and said I could play them whenever I wanted. For two years, I would come home and put on a Santana album, and then bang those drums as loud as I could. I was trying to master the Latin percussion of "Evil Ways" or "Jingo," but really I was working out my pent up aggression toward my dad.

Pat was another of my mom's long-term boyfriends. He was there through most of my late teens. Though we butted heads occasionally, he meant well and cared for us. He often shared his opinions about the economy, and offered me advice about real estate or buying tech stocks before they went through the roof. In hindsight, I wish I had followed his advice more closely.

In the fall of 1978, I started high school. It was a shock to go from a small school to a high school with over twelve-hundred hormonal teenagers. I started having anxiety attacks and, in order to cope, I continued to get stoned virtually every day through my freshman year. Getting stoned didn't take away my anxiety. In fact, it made it worse. Anxiety attacks became more frequent, especially at lunchtime, when there were hundreds of students hanging out. So, to avoid the crowded quad on campus, me and a few friends would sneak into the gym to play basketball. Sometimes I just wanted to be alone and would shoot around by myself.

When my grades started to slip in my sophomore year, I gave up pot so I could concentrate better. I poured myself into school and made a decision at fifteen years old that I would be going to college. Near the end of my sophomore year, I found beer. I started drinking on the weekends with a few of my friends.

Kelly managed to land a cushy job at the Marin Yacht Club. He made $10 an hour and got to eat steaks and party on the job. It sounded perfect and my brother got me in for a summer.

I left the Yacht Club in the fall and worked at Victoria Station for a few months, then as a busboy and valet at Dominic's Restaurant in San Rafael, and was making good money. That was also when my drinking took off. Booze got me out of my shell. Alcohol temporarily relieved my social anxieties and, after a few beers, I felt like I could talk to anyone. I was fine, until I had too much. Then, I was a blubbering idiot. During the week I went to school, studied and worked, but on the weekends, I partied hard.

Laundry Day

Saturdays were reserved for laundry and grocery shopping. We endured helping with the laundry, but it was an all-day affair. The one benefit was that we would come home with a Devil's Delight pizza from Red Boy Pizza. We also could get comics and Slurpees from the 7-eleven at Oak Manor in Fairfax.

One time when my brothers and I had come back from 7-eleven, we noticed a guy sitting at the picnic table inside the Laundromat reading the paper. But he wasn't really reading. He had torn two holes in paper and was ogling at the women doing their laundry.

"Hey butthead, what the fuck do you think you're doing?!" Kelly said, swatting the paper out of his hands. "You a peeper? Get lost, you fucking perv."

The guy insisted he was just reading the paper. My mom spoke with the owner of the Laundromat who politely asked him to leave or he would have to call the police. The guy took off and we never saw him again.

Lost Christmas Joy

I have spent many years trying to get past my hurt and anger, primarily toward my father for leaving us. As a kid from a broken family, it was hard to not hold a grudge. Especially when the rent was due, my brothers and I had to wear hand me downs and needed new shoes, and there was barely enough food in the fridge. Early on, there were times when we'd open the cupboards and they were practically bare.

People step up when needed—my dad's parents always gave my mom five hundred bucks at Christmas so we could get clothes. I took on more responsibility. Pat, my mom's new boyfriend, helped with more firewood. We made do. We survived. However, winters were difficult for me, especially around Christmas time. What once brought me great joy with food, family, presents, and at least one snowball fight, became a day I dreaded. Most of this was perpetuated by an overwhelming lack of gratitude and focus on what we didn't have, rather than being grateful for what we had. We could only afford a small four-foot tree that we propped up on a coffee table to make it look bigger. To make matters worse, our sole heat source was a wood burning stove upstairs and a toxic kerosene heater downstairs. We had no money for firewood, so my two brothers and I cut bay trees that were so green they hissed when we tried to burn them. Pat would collect scrap lumber he found in dumpsters for us to use as kindling, along with the discarded oak parquet tiles my grandpa brought us from his work. Those would burn hot enough to get the green bay going, but the tar backing and finish made some nasty smoke while the fire was starting.

I'm grateful that our home was not condemned. It had been built as a summer home and had no insulation. There was no bathroom downstairs and the single wire, ungrounded 110 amp electrical almost killed me; I was taking a bath one day, and while standing in a tub full of water, reached over to turn on the electric heater—bad idea.

Our roof was shot. It leaked like a sieve, and we had no money to get it repaired. Instead, we stapled plastic sheeting to the ceiling to collect the drips, then poked holes in the low spots and placed buckets underneath to catch the drips in four spots instead of twenty. If my dad were still around, we could have fixed all these problems. But our limited resources stared us in the face anytime we needed repairs, new clothes, or saw how many presents our friends and relatives got at Christmas. How could a mother not feel resentful about the lack of child support? How could us kids not be pissed about a father who was not there to take us to baseball, basketball, or soccer games? I missed my dad. It sucked.

Responsibility and Leadership

I now understand that I did what most oldest kids would do in a broken family—I stepped into the role of the other parent and did whatever was needed to survive and cope. It fueled my drive for control or leadership, and has followed me throughout my career and life. In some ways that is good, as I naturally wanted to take on a leadership role. But without a role model for how to lead properly, I became more of a dictator than a leader with respect to my brothers. Unfortunately this added another layer of resentment about "lost" childhood—growing up too early. This leadership style still haunts me today in my relationship with my blended family, control issues, and wanting it all done my way.

This is part of the reason why I read and study so much about leadership—I want to get better.

John Maxwell is one of the world's most prolific speakers and authors on leadership. His definition of leadership is "adding value to others." Ever since I heard that, I try to add value every day to others, to my work, and to anything I can. I seek it out.

As teenagers, my brothers and I became more disrespectful to my mom, talking back and not doing the chores she asked us to do, and just being downright rude— typical teenager stuff. But as a parent and stepparent of teenagers now, they are all angels compared to what a living hell we put our mom through back then. On one occasion she said she couldn't take it anymore and left. She was gone for over six hours. I worried that she got in a wreck and thought that maybe she actually did leave us. We were good for a while after that, but it wasn't long before she was threatening to send us off to boarding school.

One time I made her so mad she threw a cast iron skillet at me. I don't know what it was that instigated it—maybe the fact that we weren't picking up after ourselves; that we constantly fought about chores, dishes, garbage; who's turn it was—she was overwhelmed and had enough. She decided to go on strike for a whole week. She wrote out a list of what needed to be done, including all the housework, cooking, cleaning, laundry, and grocery shopping. She mapped out a budget for us and gave me $100. I made a shopping list and got busy. We did the laundry and grocery shopping and had budgeted so well that we were able to have steak *and* pizza for dinner that week. I felt like I had shown her. Unfortunately, I missed the real lesson—respect.

Between junior and senior year, Grandma Snyder wanted to have a family reunion in her home state of Nebraska. My mom thought it would be a great family trip, but it was expensive, and we were still broke.

At the time, one of the major breakfast cereal menu manufacturers was having a "Kids Fly Free" promotion. You had to collect box tops to earn points and get free or discounted air fare to anywhere in the Continental U.S. We loved it. We finally got to eat all the "good" cereals we'd wanted for so long. We had cereal for breakfast, after school, and after dinner. We had so much cereal over six months that it's a wonder I still like it. It was a perfect promotion for a single mom on a limited income with three growing boys.

Taking any kind of a trip was a big deal for our family. Even when my mom and dad were still together, the only long trips I remember were to the Grand Canyon when I was five and Disneyland with my grandparents when I was eight. Sure, we got to go on lots of camping trips and spent several summers sliding down natural water slides near my grandparents cabin in Mariposa, but there were no trips to Puerto Vallarta or Hawaii, like the vacations of some of my friends.

But our turn was coming up. Finally we were going on a summer vacation—a family reunion to Chadron Nebraska with a stop on the way to visit Grandma and Grandpa Langwell who had sold their Daly City home and were now living in Corpus Christi, Texas. Yee haw!

When the tickets finally arrived, my mom was both elated and concerned. Elated because we did it—my brothers and I had eaten enough breakfast cereal to choke a buffalo. Concerned because we had several plane transfers and layovers. One of the layovers meant she had to pay for a hotel in Minneapolis-Saint Paul which was another unexpected expense. This was not an easy pill to swallow for a mom who barely had enough money for her own ticket. Somehow she made it work.

The day came and we were off. We went to Houston first to see my grandparents in Corpus Christi. Houston was muggy enough to sweat the spots off a Cheetah. We visited with my grandparents for a day or so and spent a day swimming with the Mullet and tar globs at South Padre Island. Then we were off to Nebraska.

The flight from Houston to Kansas City seemed easy enough. My brothers and I thought it was cool how the stewardess came by to offer us free beverages. I saw that some of the adults were drinking beer or wine or cocktails. Because we had cheap tickets, we couldn't all sit together. Kelly and I had seats mid-plane while my mom and Seth sat in the back of the plane. I had a window seat. When it came time for beverage service, I nonchalantly ordered a Heineken. They served it to me. I chugged it and ordered another. I drank half and gave my brother the rest then ordered a third.

The landscape below was gorgeous from the air. When we got to Minnesota—the land of ten thousand lakes—the sunset sparkled off hundreds of ponds and lakes like tiny mirrors. It was truly a majestic sight. By the time we landed, I was pretty buzzed. My mom was already stressed about having to pay for a hotel, let alone pay for dinner. When she found out that Kelly and I were drunk, she was livid and laid into us.

We found the hotel. And sat in silent scorn through dinner.

The next day, the first leg of our flight was on a small prop plane—a puddle jumper. Up and down to Waterloo we went. No beverage service was on that flight.

The next leg, from Waterloo to Omaha was on a larger plane. My mom, once again, was further back in the plane with my youngest brother. A blonde stewardess wearing a pinstripe uniform made her way down the aisle to take drink orders. She was no more than four or five years older than me, and very cute. When she approached our row, I flashed a big smile and ordered a Heineken. I figured if I got away with it the first time, why not try it again.

"How old are you?" she asked.

"Eighteen," I lied, knowing that this was the legal drinking age in parts of the Midwest.

"Heineken it is," she smiled and proceeded down the aisle.

Kelly was sitting three rows back to my right. Looking over my shoulder, I watched as the stewardess took his order.

"And for you?" she asked.

"Heineken," he said, confidently.

"And how old are you?" she asked, raising her eyebrows.

"Eighteen," I chuckled. I couldn't believe he, too, was able to order a beer. Needless to say, both my brother and I thought we were so cool.

By the time we landed we were both pretty drunk. When my mom found out she was pissed.

My uncle met us at the airport and we began the long three hour drive from Omaha to Chadron. We drove through miles and miles of long rolling hills and lots of corn fields, with no towns or signs of civilization. I began to worry that there really isn't much else to do in Nebraska other than watch the corn grow.

Eventually we made it to Chadron. We met a slew of relatives I never knew—great aunts, uncles, cousins and second cousins. My grandma and Great-Aunt Thelma were there and so was my mom's sister, Sharon. I was hungry. After saying our hellos, my grandma made us some bologna sandwiches on white bread, then my brothers and I went downstairs to watch TV with some of our cousins. We made small talk about where we were from and all that.

Soon it was dinner time. We had burgers and hotdogs, potato salad and my grandma's signature lime Jell-O with pineapple and cottage cheese. I used to like it when I was little, but after a burger and hot dog it was enough to make me puke.

Things felt a little different at my aunt's home in Chadron, Nebraska. The cultural differences between our lifestyle and theirs, was noticeable; it felt like there were a couple elephants in the room—judgment and condemnation.

Clearly, a sharp cultural contrast existed between our hippie free love and liberal upbringing, and being raised by a single mom from California, and the morals and values of our conservative Midwest relatives. I kept noticing the differences, not only in how they talked, but more in the traditional Puritan values and gender roles they lived by; the air seemed a little thick, like a powder keg ready to blow. It came to a head when I offered to help wash the dishes after dinner as I had done for the past five years.

"Boy, dishes are woman's work," a burly, red-neck relative on my grandmother's side said as I offered to help clean up after dinner.

"Really?" I shot back with all the angst and snarkiness of a seventeen-year-old teenager. "Well my dad left when I was twelve. My mom had to get a job just to keep a roof over our head, put clothes on our back, and food on the table. We learned to help out around the house—including washing dishes!"

"No matter, son. Men don't do dishes," he sneered, like a bulldog.

Seeing this was going to go nowhere fast, I could've walked away, instead, I chose to push it to the next level.

"Well, since we ain't got land to tend nor cows to milk, I reckon getting our hands wet with a little dishwater is the California equivalent of helping out around the house." I snapped back.

"Don't get smart with me boy."

"Boy?! I ain't your boy."

"You're a little pansy—doing dishes…" he hurled the insult, while flopping his wrists.

"Excuse me?! A pansy?!" I clenched my jaw, my knuckles white as I made a fist.

Now I was getting pissed. *Who was this fucking redneck, hillbilly to tell me what is right and wrong?!* I felt my blood boiling. "Well that may be how you were raised—but it wasn't how I was. So, if you have a problem with it…" I leaned in, glancing at the counter for a pot or something heavy to knock some sense into his thick skull.

"What's going on here?!" Overhearing the commotion, my mom stepped in to defend me.

"This guy called me a pansy for doing dishes…says it's woman's work."

"Well I think you owe my son an apology then," she said to "Uncle Ed."

"I don't owe him nothing. If anything, he should apologize to me for disrespecting his elders."

"He's just helping out. Ain't nothing wrong with that," my mom said as calmly as she could. "Why don't you both apologize to each other? It doesn't mean you have to agree with one another—just be civil."

We apologized; agreeing to disagree and moved on.

I wanted a beer. I had spotted a small grocery/liquor store/deli on the way up the hill. So I went for a walk, found the store, bought a six-pack of Lowenbrau and went back to the house to watch some more TV while drinking beer with my brothers and younger cousins.

The next day was the big family reunion. It was to be held at a VFW in Chadron, Nebraska. I would have rather watched corn grow. We went down early with my uncle to help set up. Twelve tables were set out. We placed red and white checkered cloths on the tables, and placed ninety-six chairs around them.

My brothers, and second cousins went outside while the adults finished setting up inside.

On the way out I spotted a jug of Gallo wine that sat on the kitchen floor. I grabbed it and snuck it out the back door. Kelly, two of our second cousins, and I passed it around, each taking a big gulp. It tasted nasty, but we got a little buzz. I returned the jug to where I found it and we wandered over to a nearby park.

I don't remember much about the big reunion, but the next day we all got to drive up to The Black Hills of South Dakota to see Mount Rushmore. The contrast of rich black earth against the vibrant green meadows teeming with free range wild bison was spectacular. We saw Mt. Rushmore then went to the Rushmore caves five miles further up the road. I had never been in a cavern before. The air was still, musty and very cool. Massive stalactites hung from the ceiling like earthly chandeliers. It was truly breathtaking.

High School Senior

I was doing well in school, making good money, and was no longer a virgin. I began to feel a little more confident in my abilities. All through school, I had hung my sense of identity on praise and validation for doing a good job. When my grades started slipping in my freshman year, I felt like I was a failure. When I started working in the restaurant business, instant cash, instant gratification and praise fueled my sense of worth. I chased that immediate gratification, for several years. An inner will to succeed propelled me forward to continue to grow, improve, and make the most out of my life. If I stumbled, I got back up. If someone said something couldn't be done, I became determined to prove them wrong. I had yet to learn humility, but that would change.

I graduated in June of 1982 and was off to the races— working, making good money and partying. I was an adult and felt on top of the world. Things were going so well that I became cocky. Nothing will knock you to your knees faster than a runaway ego coupled with booze and drugs. I started drinking nearly every day. My mom was nice enough to let me use her truck to get to and from work, but I had no real restrictions. Basically, I didn't always come home right after work. Instead, I went out partying. Worried that I wasn't lying dead in a ditch somewhere, she would stay up long past her bedtime waiting for me to come home safely. After the second or third time of waiting up past 1 a.m., she relented to my teenage selfishness, and decided to hope for the best, no longer staying up 'til the wee hours of the morning.

I must've had a guardian angel watching over me, because somehow I made it through that self-destructive period alive. I also went through a phase where I was snorting cocaine regularly, but fortunately got sick of it before it became a huge addiction. In hindsight, I was so selfish and self-centered; years later I apologized to my mom for causing her so much worry.

That fall, after a quick adventure to the US festival with some high school friends, I started College of Marin.

Even though I had the GPA and SAT scores to go to Berkeley or Stanford, I didn't want the expense. So I decided to go to College of Marin for a year while I figured out where I would go next. Initially, I wanted to get some of my general education classes done and thought I would pursue a degree in Architectural design but I quickly realized it was not for me. I saw that drafting would soon be done by computers and I did not have the patience nor creativity to be a draftsman or an architect.

I had made up my mind. I decided to apply to San Diego State University. I wanted a business degree, but that program was impacted. So I applied as undeclared and was accepted for the fall semester in 1983. Prior to that, my grandmother had asked me where I was planning on going to school before I chose SDSU. I told her that I had narrowed it down to San Diego State and Chico State.

"Well why don't you just pick the two biggest party schools in California!" she quipped.

How did she know that? I thought. My grandmother was a sharp woman.

"Well the weather certainly is nice in San Diego," she added, gently encouraging me to go to San Diego instead of Chico. I made the right choice—after all who wouldn't want to live ten minutes from the beach in a college town where the weather is seventy degrees year round and the girls are pretty?

Chapter 9
The Wheelie King

Three years earlier, in the summer of 1979, someone gave us a unicycle. Neither my brothers nor I knew how to ride it. By the end of the summer, we all had mastered it. At first we could only go a short distance. We'd take turns trying to balance and then pedal without falling. Just like the pogo sticks, we'd ride that thing anywhere we could. One of the most challenging spots to ride it was along the thin dirt trail carved into the hill along the back edge of our property. It took a few times, but again my brothers and I figured it out. Kelly mastered it first, then Seth. I enjoyed it, but not nearly as much as my brothers. By the end of the following summer, I had my license and was working a lot. That unicycle became Seth's primary mode of transportation before he got his motorcycle license. He rode it everywhere. He even made the front page of a local paper. I used to joke that we were so poor we couldn't afford bikes. All we had was a unicycle— one wheel, and we had to share it.

Later Seth took up mountain biking. He'd ride all over Mt. Tam, fearlessly bombing down steep narrow trails. But his claim to fame was riding wheelies—he could ride them for miles.

I was away at college, but heard the story several times from him and his friends—the story of his epic ride that solidified his title as the "Wheelie King."

As it goes...

One day, Seth mounted his mountain bike and popped a wheelie at the edge of Samuel P. Taylor Park in Lagunitas, and he continued riding along Sir Francis Drake Blvd., past Forest Knolls, San Geronimo, and the long stretch along the golf course. A line of cars slowed and honked to show their support. As he approached Woodacre, a Marin County

Sheriff found out from his friends what was going on and followed behind, offering protection as a Sheriff escort while Seth pedaled up and over White's Hill from Woodacre to Fairfax. He was still going—down White's Hill, around the turns, waving at drivers who honked their horns in encouragement. I'm sure he wore a confident grin from ear to ear, passing Lefty Gomez field where he played soccer, waving to the kids playing soccer, "Beep! Beep! I'm the Wheelie King!"

He rounded the last curve and set down his front tire when on the flats in Fairfax.

"Yeah! That's what I'm talking about!" he waved as the caravan of cars passed. Drivers waved and honked. For those that were there and his close friends, that story would be told a hundred times. Word spread, he was officially known as the Wheelie King—a moniker that, among his friends, will live forever. Even though I wasn't there to witness it, my brother always had an air of confidence, charm, and wit that made people want to be around him.

Yes, my brother was an adrenaline junkie. Whether doing back-scratchers off cornices in Tahoe while snowboarding, fearlessly flying down steep trails on his mountain bike, riding wheelies for miles, or skydiving, he loved anything that was fast.

He also loved soccer. In U-16 soccer, he would dribble the length of the field as fast as he could and score three to five goals a game. He just outran everyone in the opposing team. It was a sight to see, he made it look easy.

He was a free spirit, with a sharp wit and a heart of a champion. I was proud to have him as my brother.

Later, he inspired a family friend along with several others to take up take up mountain bike racing. But sadly, one of his close friends (a mountain biking legend in his own right) had a terminal illness. There wasn't a damn thing anybody could do about it. His friend lost the battle.

After his friend's passing my brother dropped into deep mourning. He turned to poetry and his journal to process his inner turmoil.

Here's one of his poems, called "The Rain."

"The Rain"

As the rain falls from the sky,
I think and wonder why?

The freshness of the air is brought
forth by rain, assuring me that
I am not insane.

The raindrops fall from the sky
like a tear drop from my eye.
Thinking of what I have done
will there be any sun?

Because when it rains it pours
And what you have done in yours.

So when it rains, feel no pain
And open your eyes and look to the sky,
and ask yourself why,

and what can I do to find my way through
This endless maze without being crazed?

and unleash the good and do away with the bad
so on rainy days I'll never be sad.

Seth Langwell - 1992

Chapter 10
San Diego State

The big day arrived. I was going away to college. At nineteen, I felt like a high roller, even with only $1,300 in my pocket. I packed as much as I could into the trunk and back seat of my mom's 1980 Honda Accord, and we headed off for San Diego. We took the scenic route along Highway 101 and Highway 1 through Big Sur, Monterey, Santa Cruz, and Santa Barbara before cutting across to I-5 in Los Angeles. Fourteen hours later, we pulled up Montezuma Avenue to The El Conquistador Dorm at San Diego State University.

I was in awe. When I had come down six weeks earlier for a brief visit to check it out, it was still in the process of being renovated. It had been trashed by previous students and had a reputation as one of the biggest party dorms off campus. Now it was newly painted and had lush landscaping outside, making it look like a nine-story hotel rather than an off-campus dorm.

As we parked and went inside, I kept thinking, *I can't believe I am doing this. I am actually going away to college.* Up to that point, nobody in our family had gone away to college. For some, that's not a big deal. But as a poor kid who grew up in the San Geronimo Valley of West Marin, it was a very big deal to me.

We approached the front desk to check in. An elderly woman, Betty, sat there organizing mounds of paper. I introduced myself, and Betty said I would have to wait two hours before I could have my keys.

"You are welcome to store your stuff here while you wait," she said, pointing to a storage area behind the front desk.

"Thank you." I said, disappointed that I'd have to wait two more hours to get my room after the long drive to get there.

"Then I'll give you and your mom a brief tour of the facility," Betty continued.

"That would be lovely," my mom said.

My mom helped me unload and store my few belongings—clothes, a pillow and blankets—and then Betty gave us a tour.

Off the lobby, was a recreation room with a pool table and two ping-pong tables. It also had laundry facilities and vending machines. Down another hallway was a study area with several desks. Opposite the entry was the cafeteria where I could have three meals a day. Betty pointed out the pool and sauna and then mentioned that I would also have a weekly maid. I smiled, looking at my mom as she rolled her eyes.

The tour was brief and we were getting hungry so my mom and I decided to drive down the street for a burrito at a local taco stand. When we returned, there was still over an hour left before I could get my keys. Rather than sit around with my mom, I gave her a hug and kiss goodbye. In hindsight I probably should've had her wait to see my room, but I was itching for my freedom. She understood.

After my mom left, I decided to take a quick tour of the campus again. It was huge, but what I remember most is that there were so many good looking, sun kissed college students everywhere.

I familiarized myself with as much as I could, and then returned to the dorm to get my keys and go check out my room. The previous receptionist was gone and the site manager, Shirley, was now behind the desk. She was a sweet young black woman who was very welcoming and professional. She gave me the property map and a stack of papers with the meal times and my rental agreement. She reminded me that rent was due on the 1st of the month and, a $50 late fee would be assessed after the fifth.

"Room #902," she said as she handed me the keys. "Elevator's there. Top floor. Turn right. First room on the right."

Still in awe that this was actually happening, but not yet sure what to expect, I thanked her and headed to the elevator. I pushed the button and took the elevator up to the ninth floor.

The carpet inside had been stripped and not yet replaced. It reeked of beer and puke. *Uh-oh*, I thought, *what am I getting into?* I figured they were still finalizing construction. I later found out that it would be completed over the next two weeks prior to school starting. I was early. I wanted to get settled in.

The elevator door opened. I entered the tile lobby of the ninth floor and turned right. I unlocked the door of room #902 and entered. It was bright with a view that extended all the way to the football field across campus and down the hill.

"Wow!" I exclaimed aloud.

Clothes were strewn everywhere. Obviously my roommate had already been here a while. On the desk were a pair of Black Nike basketball shoes. They were huge—probably size fifteens.

Cool, I thought, *they roomed me with someone who likes basketball.* On the nightstand was a picture of a very large black person. I looked closer and couldn't tell if it was a guy or a girl. I didn't know what to think. I felt like Sherlock Holmes, searching the room for more clues about my roommate. Then I got my question answered. On the counter next to the wash basin was a tube of Dep hair gel and a big white and blue box of Tampax!

"What the fuck?" I muttered as I laughed to myself. *Guess they put me in a room with one of the players from the San Diego State University women's basketball team.* I knew it was a co-ed dorm, but I seriously doubted that they wanted a guy in a room with a woman. But then again, I wasn't sure. Maybe this was taking desegregation to an entirely new level...I doubted that. I left and went downstairs and told the manager that there must've been a mistake.

She looked over the application and laughed.

"I guess they thought you were a woman. Your writing looks like Sharon, plus since you indicated that you like basketball, they thought it was a good fit."

"Yeah, I love basketball. But rooming with a woman probably isn't a good idea."

"Sorry about that," she chuckled. "Yeah even though it's a co-ed dorm, we don't have men and women sharing rooms or suites."

She gave me another room assignment. I took the key and headed back upstairs to check out my new room. It had great light and overlooked the pool—perfect for a young college student.

Because the ninth floor was supposed to be the quiet floor, and likely not a first choice for many students, there was an eclectic mix of serious students, a wide diversity of international students, and the SDSU women's basketball team.

We called ourselves the United Nations floor. I had a lot of great times living there—watching movies, trips to Tijuana and Rosarito Beach, playing soccer and Frisbee in the hallway with my roommate, and, as with most college dorms, lots of drinking and carousing. I was a late bloomer, and as a young college kid full of booze and hormones, I was not very scrupulous.

Most of this is a blur because I was literally drunk for the first full semester of college.

I was getting grants and financial aid, and my grandparents were giving me $200 a month. So I didn't need to work, yet. I managed to make it to class and successfully "crashed" several prerequisite classes so I could declare a business major. I struggled the first semester. Partying was more important than studying. I fell behind quickly and became depressed. Booze didn't help.

Early in that first semester, I ran into a childhood friend, Dion. I didn't even know he was going to school there. He was living out of his VW Bus.

I wasn't supposed to, but I snuck him in and let him crash on my floor for a month. In the morning, I'd grab a cup of coffee from the cafeteria, and then loan him my meal card for breakfast and lunch so he could have enough food for the day. Staff eventually caught on and politely informed me that he had to go.

It was around this time that my alcoholism really took off. My grades suffered. I couldn't even concentrate enough to complete a basic English class in college. Even my friends that had visited and partied with me saw how out of control my drinking was and suggested that I may want to slow down. I got to a place that once I started drinking, I couldn't stop. One day, I had gotten seriously sick and went to the school doctor.

"How much do you drink?" he asked.

"A few a day," I said, averting his eyes.

"Every day?" he asked, looking at me sideways.

"Yeah," I replied, as if it wasn't a big deal—everyone in college drinks, right?

"Have a seat," he said, pointing to the exam chair, while he checked my vitals and pressed on my abdomen and back. "Your liver is enlarged—it's twice the size it should be. I think you're drinking more than you say. You should cut it back or stop," he said, in a serious tone, scribbling a few notes in my file.

"Well I do drink a six-pack or so on the weekends," I added, knowing it was a complete lie—I was drinking nearly a case on the weekend and about a six-pack every night.

"Well, drink more water and cut back on your drinking. Then you should feel better," he said without any condemnation.

This was the first time I grasped that alcohol was adversely affecting my health. That didn't stop me, though. I left and headed straight to a frat party and got hammered.

Usually after school, I'd try to get back to the dorm to study before dinner and all the partying. Two or three days in one week I noticed a tall blonde walking home from school at the same time as me. I had never met her before, but she lived in the same dorm. I was still shy, especially when I didn't have any beer. The first time, I just glanced over. The second time when I looked, she saw me and smiled. I returned a nervous smile and looked away. *What do I say? How do I break the ice? What if she gets in the elevator the same time?* I was a nervous wreck. She walked faster. By the time I entered the lobby, she was already gone. A day or so later, it happened again. I smiled. She smiled back. Only this time, she slowed down. We entered the building at the same time, but said nothing. *Why does it have to be so awkward to talk to a girl?* She pushed the up button for the elevator and we stood there in awkward silence, waiting. She broke the ice by introducing herself.

"Hi, I'm Teri," she said, extending her hand.

"I'm Shawn. Nice to meet you."

The doors opened and we stepped in. We then made small talk for thirty seconds as we stood alone in the elevator.

The following weekend was Halloween. Several of us dressed up and had a party on the ninth floor. I grew tired of it and went downstairs to watch a movie on the downstairs lobby TV with some other dorm mates.

Teri walked into the lobby wearing camouflage pants and thick black eye make-up and black lipstick. She held up a paper bag and waved and winked.

"Wanna party?" she asked, pursing her lips.

"Sure," I said without hesitation. We ended up dating until winter break. We didn't date for long but when she wasn't working or we weren't studying, we spent every minute together.

Midterms were nearly over and I wanted to go home for Thanksgiving. I ran into Dion, who said he was driving home for Thanksgiving. He wanted to know if I wanted to go with him, and split the cost of gas. Another friend from the dorm, Jim, who lived in Brisbane, also decided to join us.

It started out well. We piled into Dion's VW bus and headed west on Highway 8, then north to the 405. Just past Long Beach, traffic backed up but it was no big deal—we had plenty of beer for the ride and we were on top of the world. As we rolled along the 405 we laughed, drank, listened to music, and recounted stories from the first couple of semesters at school.

Traffic started backing up again at Highway 5 near downtown Los Angeles. Thirteen miles north of Burbank, in Castaic, we broke down. Fortunately, Jim had a godfather who lived nearby. He called his godfather from a payphone, who agreed to come pick us up and let us stay with him and his wife for the night.

After they had gone to bed, we found their liquor cabinet and helped ourselves to some cocktails.

The next morning Jim's uncle was kind enough to help us get a rental car. I don't remember much else, other than I got really, really drunk and threw up, making the rest of the ride miserable for the other two.

We dropped Jim off in Brisbane, and I laid down in the back seat while Dion continued on to Woodacre. It was raining and nearly dark when Dion and I finally arrived at my house. The car reeked of my puke, and I was still pretty wasted.

Dion parked the car, grabbed my bag out of the trunk, and aided me up the steps, one at a time. The dog barked as I staggered in through the door. My mom and brothers were shocked to see me so wasted; I was covered in puke and drunk as a skunk.

Dion said hi and bye quickly to my mom and brothers. My mom thanked him for getting us home safely and he left.

In hindsight, that was the first time I recall being that wasted in front of my family.

We returned without incident, but even when I got back to school, my life seemed to be spiraling out of control quickly. I was finding it increasingly more difficult to concentrate while studying; I often needed to read chapters several times for the material to sink in. I was getting frustrated. All my life I had done well in school, and now I felt like a failure. I wanted to run away from it all.

I couldn't wait for the semester to be over and to go home again for winter break. I pushed through my finals and, just before the end of the semester, Teri decided it would be better to stop dating. *When will it end?*, I thought. At first I was crushed—I really liked her. We had a lot of fun together, but we were only twenty and had a whole life ahead of us. So, we said goodbye.

A college buddy had offered to let me use his car for the break. I was stoked—I had wheels for the winter break! The next day, I packed up my stuff, grabbed a case of beer and headed home.

By the time I hit the Grapevine, I was so drunk, I had to pull over at a rest stop to sober up.

I finally made it home safely and was glad I didn't have to deal with school for a few weeks. I reconnected with a bunch of high school buddies and spent most of the time partying. Alcohol was beginning to rule my life.

One night, I went out dancing with a bunch of friends and ended up getting really drunk. When it was time to go, my friends, Joe and Antony, implored me to come with them, but I insisted on staying. I thought I might get lucky—what a joke—instead I was arrested for being drunk and disorderly in public. You'd think that would be a wakeup call...nope. I wasn't done yet.

Just before the end of the break, I got a phone call. It was my ex-girlfriend.

It caught me off-guard, we had broken up. *Why was she calling? How did she get my number?*

After a bit of small talk, she cut to the chase—"I'm pregnant."

"What? How? You had protection. We haven't been together for a while. How do you know it's mine?" I said, reeling at the shocking news.

"It must've been the first time—on Halloween—my birth control must not have been at the right level," she explained.

"How far along?" I asked.

"Ten weeks—I'm almost at the end of the first trimester."

"Oh my God!" I paused, trying to process all this. *What's the right thing to do? To say? What does she want to do? Being a dad would be cool. I want kids, but I'm not ready to be a dad. Is this the woman I want to be with? Does that mean we have to get married? What if she doesn't want to keep it? What if she wants an abortion? How would I deal with that?*

"So what does that mean? Do you want to keep it? We're broken up, so should we get married?"

"No—no. I've decided to get an abortion, but I don't have the money. I need $200."

I felt like I was punched in the gut.

"Uh…okay. Are you sure it's mine?" I asked, even though I knew I probably shouldn't.

"Yes, I'm sure it's yours! I haven't been with anyone since you," she replied, offended at my insinuation that she'd slept with someone else.

I looked at the floor, trying to think of the right thing say the right thing to do. "Okay. Are you sure you don't want to keep it? We can get married and make it work. Even if you don't want to be together I will help support you and the baby." I offered, unsure that was what I really wanted.

"That's kind of you, but I have made up my mind. I have an appointment next week. Can you send me $200?"

"Yeah. I can come down early."

"No. I need to do this on my own."

"Wow—okay." I said, feeling completely cut out. *She only wants my money*, I thought. "I'll come back early and give you the money next week," I had already talked myself into becoming a dad and, at the time, was relieved when she said no. But was taken aback when she wanted nothing from me except $200.

"Can you just mail it? It would be better." I paused, feeling completely defeated. *Is this really happening?*

"Okay, sure. Where do you want me to send it?" I gave in.

I got the address, hung up the phone and went straight to my mom and cried my eyes out. When I returned to school, I was numb. I don't recall ever talking to my ex-girlfriend about it again.

I returned to school after the Christmas break with a determination to be more serious. I knuckled down and starting doing well.

My report card arrived shortly after I returned and it had a couple W's on it, the equivalent of F's. In high school I had good grades. Now, I was barely at a "C" average.

I felt like a complete failure. I had dreamed of college—to get away from home, to earn my independence, and to get an education and make something of myself. Now I felt like I was letting myself and my family down. Even though they supported me emotionally, this was all on me. So much of my identity all through grammar school and high school was tied to doing well in school and getting praise and recognition. I was responsible. I picked up the slack when my dad left and helped my mom around the house. I had good income from restaurant work and had become relatively independent at an early age. On the outside I may have appeared successful, but inside I was a mess. Now with a crappy report card, an enlarged liver, the morning shakes, and coming off a break up and abortion, I ran to the bottle and cocaine for escape. It didn't work. It only made me more depressed.

One evening, I walked to the end of the balcony on the ninth floor. It was late spring and the air was warm. The sky was lit with a late afternoon glow but inside I was a wreck—dark, broken, crazy. The thought of jumping crossed my mind for a moment. My fingers curled around the iron railing as I looked over the edge of the balcony. *No, it's too high,* I thought. I walked down the stairwell to the sixth floor. A dumpster sat at the edge of the parking lot seventy feet below. *Fuck it!* I thought. *My life is a waste. I can't do this anymore.* Thoughts of my mom, my brothers, and grandparents ran through my head. *I can't fail. I'm letting everyone down.* My heart raced as I grabbed the railing and rocked like I was going to hurl myself over. One…two…three…. I started to throw my legs over the black steel railing. Instead, I pushed away, falling on my ass. I crawled to my knees and banged my forehead on the cool hard concrete balcony and sobbed. *No! Not now! Suck it up…you can get through this. This is a cowardly thing to do. Man up.*

Then, like a guardian angel, one of my dorm mates happened to come up the stairwell and, recognizing my despair, talked me off the ledge.

"Dude, I know how you feel. I've been there before. In fact, the last time I did blow, I got to that same place. It will pass. Come on. Let's go," he said pointing to the hallway.

"I know. But I really want to jump." And I did. But now, the need was different. "Not to kill myself, but I really want to jump into that dumpster—there's a mattress in there. It couldn't hurt that bad." The desire to jump become an adventure rather than a depressing half-hearted, cocaine induced suicidal muse.

Looking over the railing, he said, "Yeah, that would be fun. But this is too high. Let's do it from the third floor. C'mon. I'll jump with you."

We walked three stories down, then eyed the dumpster from the third floor. It still looked too high, so we went to the second, then without hesitation he grabbed the railing and leapt over.

I followed a few seconds later.

"Is that better?" he asked.

"Yeah."

"Good, let's go get a beer."

So we left for a frat party down the street.

By the spring semester of 1985, I was growing tired of the dorm and needed to get serious about school. Dion needed a roommate, so I decided to move in with him for a semester.

The apartment was spacious and affordable, but like many apartments in San Diego, it had roaches. Dion and I always laughed at how fast they'd scurry out of sink and the across the counter when we flipped on the kitchen light at night.

Dion is a smart guy, and was very serious about getting his degree. That helped me stay focused—for a while. With some of my general education out of the way I was now taking business classes like Business Law and Accounting.

I studied my ass off for my accounting final. I got some meth and pulled an all-nighter, reading and re-reading my notes. Wide-eyed, I walked into my final the next morning and was half way done. I excused myself to use the restroom, snorted another line of meth and went back to finish the two hundred question test in half the time allotted. I ended up getting one hundred ninety-eight out of two hundred correct.

This was probably the only time doing drugs worked. It lulled me into arrogance. For the time being, I was on the right track, and felt great about it. After that semester, I stopped the meth and though I was still drinking, I felt like I had it under control.

It had been a while since I dated. One afternoon, one of my roommate's co-workers, Jenny, had stopped by to see him for a little late afternoon fun. Since he was gone, I had agreed to take his place. We drank and got busy, then she pulled out some toys, including a pair of handcuffs.

I had never been handcuffed before, but she assured me that she'd take them off whenever I wanted. So I agreed to let her do it. The thought of being controlled was hot and, at first, I liked it. Then she started getting more sadistic and it freaked me out.

"Take 'em off!" I shouted.

"No, take it like a man! I'm not done with you!" she barked back, straddling me.

I know for some this may sound like an exciting story of a college sexual escapade—and at first it was. But it stopped being fun when she ignored me and continued to take me. In hindsight, I was violated.

She finished and left me there cuffed to the bed. I was so pissed, I literally started bouncing and shaking the bed trying to get free. She stood there watching as I struggled. Eventually, I calmed down enough to have her unlock me.

Around that time, Dion came home. She opened the door, and left without another word.

Chapter 11
Alvarado Street

In the fall, I moved to Alvarado Street. I felt like I had arrived. It was a very nice condo one mile away from SDSU. I shared a three bedroom condo with two new roommates, Don and Kelly. My room was sunny and large. The complex also had a pool and Jacuzzi, which became one of my favorite places to hang out and drink. Both of my roommates had cars, so we were able to get out to the movies, the beach, Tijuana, Rosarito Beach, or an occasional happy hour. One of my roommates was a young, attractive, well-endowed blonde woman who loved to drink like I did. Though she had a boyfriend, we would often hit up happy hour and down a pitcher or two of margaritas. We kissed once, but nothing else, even though I wanted more. Her boyfriend was huge and would have kicked my ass if he found out.

One night, we all went to the local bar and restaurant where I worked to celebrate my roommate's birthday. We got hammered. I had become friends with some of the cooks who did meth and got hooked on that for a short bit. We all got pretty wasted. I did meet a young attractive woman there who was also celebrating her birthday. We immediately hit it off. That night there was lots of laughing and a whole lot of drinking. The next thing I remember I was being carried out of the bar and thrown into someone's backseat, along with my new friend. We were all going back to our place. I don't remember much else. I awoke the next morning with this young woman next to me. As I meandered downstairs to make some coffee I noticed the entire living room floor covered with sleeping bodies. It became a classic drunken relationship. She was wild, and so was I.

College was a lot of fun, until it stopped being fun. Booze helped for a while, but it stopped working. On slow nights at the restaurant where I worked, I'd goof off in the kitchen. The cooks would toss me cherry tomatoes, cucumbers, and cooked prawns from across the room that I'd catch in my mouth like a dog getting a treat. One night I asked if I could have a couple prawns. The head cook said no.

"C'mon," I pleaded. "I'm hungry."

"Okay," he said, "but you have to bark like a seal, then I'll toss you one."

"Fine," so I raised my neck back and clapped my hands and barked like a seal. He tossed me a prawn which I caught in my mouth.

"Another," I said, then barked louder—"ARR! ARR!" I clapped my hands and barked just like the seals at the zoo at feeding time. Now picture in slow motion a big baby-faced chef with a tall chef hat tossing a prawn twenty feet across the kitchen to a skinny twenty-one-year-old college student barking like a seal....it was a perfect toss, *I got this* I thought. In the corner of my eye, as I caught the perfectly tossed prawn, the manager came inside the door behind me. *"Ru-Roh,"* I muttered under my breath.

"Bad move," he said. "You're fired." That was the end of that.

Going Downhill Fast

My girlfriend had let me borrow her car a few times while she worked. After showing up late and drunk one too many times, she dumped me. Once again, my world was crumbling.

I had no job and my resources were limited, so to numb my feelings, I resorted to drinking cheap jug wine. For maximum effect and to mask the taste, I gulped it from a thirty-two ounce tumbler filled with a few ice cubes, twenty ounces of Gallo white and a splash of 7-Up. It got me drunk fast, but that crap gave me a wicked headache, so I later switched to rum and Coke. It tasted better, but still gave me a nasty hangover.

One spring day, while soaking in the hot tub and gawking at some of the gorgeous tanned women at the pool, I saw a couple college students walk over to the Pepsi vending machine, rock it and shake loose a couple of free Pepsis. I didn't really give it a second though until two days later. It was early evening, and I had already drank about half a fifth of rum. I sat in the tub with a half of a tumbler full of rum and Coke—I was already drunk. For no reason, I got up and tried to shake the soda machine. It was way too heavy from my skinny 160 lb. frame. I couldn't budge it. So I jumped up to grab the top of the vending machine, and pushed against the wall with my feet. It rocked. I pushed harder—too hard. The 1,000 lb. machine rocked past the tipping point, I lost my balance and tried to catch my fall on a brick wall where the BBQ area was. The machine slammed down on my right hand and nearly tore off my right finger.

"OH MY GOD!!! SOMEBODY HELP ME!" I screamed as loud as I could, looking at my mangled hand.

Blood dripped down my arm. I could see bone. "Help!"

A neighbor overheard my scream and came to help. I was still in shock and beside myself. I could barely tell him my name or what happened.

"Where do you live?"

"I don't know." In my drunken stupor, I couldn't even remember where my condo was.

"That, way…" I pointed to the front of the complex. Fortunately, my roommate was home and he drove me to the hospital two blocks down the street.

The next thing I remember is laying in the ER with my hand bandaged, held above my head to stop the bleeding and screaming, "Someone get me some fucking pain killers!"

I was that guy. My blood alcohol content was at .20%. Experts say that a .40% to .50% BAC is fatal; I was already half dead. There was no way in hell they could give me any pain meds. I could have died.

Regardless, the pain was excruciating. The duty nurse told me to shut up and that a surgeon was on their way from Los Angeles.

I passed in and out of consciousness. When the surgeon finally arrived, I vaguely remember him telling me that what I did was stupid and could have killed me.

I have no idea how long the surgery was. When I came to, the phone by my bed rang. It was my mom. I broke down, but was more concerned about the fact that this was going to cost a lot of money, and we only had a $500 emergency insurance policy. I said goodbye to my mom and pressed the nurse call button. "I need more pain meds," I told her.

"You just had some. You have to wait."

The doctor came in shortly afterward to check on me. "You are lucky—I had to remove hundreds of tiny paint chips from your wound. I also had to reattach several nerves and tendons. You have fifty-six stitches in your hand. The metacarpal near your right knuckle sheared off, but I was able to reattach it with a stainless steel pin that will hold it in place until it heals."

"Will I be able to use it again?" I asked, worried that I had royally fucked up.

"Yes, if you keep it clean. You need to soak it and change the dressing twice a day for two weeks. If you don't keep it clean, gangrene could set in and you may lose your whole hand. Here are directions and a cleaning solution to keep the wound dressed, a prescription for an antibiotic, and Vicodin for pain as needed. Also, don't drink with the Vicodin. Sleep with it elevated as best as possible. Any questions?"

"How long will it take to heal?"

"About six weeks. If you follow directions, you should regain full use of your finger. It may be stiff, but better than the alternative right?" he said, raising his bushy eyebrows.

"Yeah. Thanks Doc."

"You're welcome. Take care of yourself."

He left, and the pain grew more intense. I was preoccupied with having to go into debt to be in the hospital. I was coming down. I pressed the nurse call button again.

"I want out," I said with a firm resolve, even though I knew I was in no shape to take care of myself.

"The doctor said you should stay overnight, while we monitor you," the nurse said, shaking her head.

"I can't afford it. I want to go now," I insisted.

The nurse did her best to convince me to stay. Ultimately, I got my discharge papers and my prescription, and then headed home. My hand was throbbing, and I hated pain pills. I wanted…no, I *needed* a drink.

I dropped off my supplies at the condo and headed straight for Kelly's Pub—one of my favorite Irish bars. *Nothing a few pitchers of beer can't help.* I am sure I made a complete ass out of myself, bragging about my accident. Either I got 86'd or ran out of money, and I staggered back down the hill toward our condo. The hill was steep. I kept losing my balance and falling into the bushes, banging my bloodied hand on the sharp branches. I stumbled a few more steps, then, feeling sick, leaned into the bushes to puke. I lost my balance and fell into the shrubs and passed out.

It was mid-day when I came to. I had fallen face first into my own puke, and everything stunk. This was not what I pictured my life would be at twenty-one. I was off the rails, heading for a cliff. Thank God it didn't end there.

It would take several weeks for me to heal. Over the next several days, I treated the wound and changed the dressing as directed. But I was very uncomfortable. I hated the Vicodin, so I drank my pain away instead. My grand dream to be the first in my family to go away and complete a college education was quickly evaporating. Now I couldn't even write, and was failing school. I was nearly broke and felt helpless, and I knew my only option was to drop out.

As I sat in my room feeling sorry for myself, I spotted a pink wallet card on my bookshelf that my dad had sent me a while back. It was the Prayer of Salvation. A couple years earlier, my dad had become a born-again Christian, which enabled him to stop drinking and using drugs. I don't recall the exact words, but here's the gist, as best I can recall:

God, I know that I have made decisions based on self-will that have hurt me. I have not always placed you first. I now realize that of my own will I am nothing, and that through your son, Jesus, I can be forgiven and redeemed. I choose now to accept Jesus into my heart. He died on the cross and paid the ultimate penalty for my sin. I am eternally grateful for his sacrifice and now offer myself to you to do with as you wish. Relieve me of my sin and guide my path so that I may better do your will. Thy will, not mine, be done. In your son's loving name I pray. Amen.

I bristled at the thought of religion, but the words struck a chord—I was broken—those words offered a ray of hope.

My grandparents had been giving me $200 a month for school costs, which was nearly enough to cover my rent. But that was money to help pay for my living expenses while in school. I couldn't take their money if I wasn't going to stay in school. I had to call and let them know what happened and ask them to stop sending me money. I took a deep breath and called my grandma. I explained my situation. She understood, but insisted on helping—

"Well you'll still need money to live," she said.

"Yeah, but Grandma, I don't feel right taking your money if I'm not in school. I am probably going to have to go home, anyway," I said, staring at the floor, holding back the tears.

"Ok, but I'll send you one last check to help with expenses. I hope you get better soon," she said with all the love anyone could ever want from a grandmother.

Her check arrived a few days later and covered most of my rent but I had no other income and resorted to writing bad checks at the local liquor store and 7-11 to get booze, peanut butter and jelly, and basic convenience food.

Even with a broken finger, I had to get work. I found a few leads in the local paper and took the bus to drop off applications. A few days later, one of the restaurants on Hotel Circle called me back for an interview. I asked my friend Duane if I could borrow his car after class.

"Sure. No problem. Don't wreck it, and I need it back tonight," he said, flipping me the keys.

The interview went well, considering my past restaurant experience, but they didn't want to take a risk of hiring me with a broken hand. They asked me to come back when my hand was healed. I was bummed. But really, what was I thinking? Did I really expect that I could get a job with a broken hand? Well, yeah, I did.

School was over for the weekend which meant, party time at the frats! I drove back to campus and parked Duane's car in the lower school lot, then proceeded to get wasted at a TGIF party at one of the frats. Frat parties were a college kid's dream—it only cost $5 for all the beer you could drink, they usually had a decent live band, and there were always several scantily clad college beauties there. In fact, the women outnumbered the guys nearly six to four, and were not shy. But I was alone and uncomfortable, so I drank more, faster to overcome my social anxiety. I drank five to seven beers in an hour or so, and still felt too awkward to ask anyone to dance. So I staggered back down the hill to my condo and passed out around 5 p.m.

Wake Up Call

"Wake up, asshole! Where's my fucking car?!!!" my friend Duane, shouted while kicking the edge of my bed. "Where's my car?!"

I was so wasted, I could hardly keep my eyes open, let alone answer him.

"Let's go, dude!" he growled, slapping me across the cheeks. "Wake up! Dude, where's my fucking car?!" Duane demanded again, punching me in the shoulder.

"Huh? What?"

"You heard me, dick-wad. Where's my fucking car?"

"Uh—mmm, at school…parking lot…" I slurred.

"Where, at school?! Which lot?" he pressed, getting more irritated.

My eyes closed again—head spinning—I just wanted to sleep it off.

"Lower lot…" I mumbled, just wishing I could pass out again.

"Hey, asshole! I loaned you my car. I need it. Show me where it is," he ordered as he picked me up and pulled me to my feet. I could barely stand up straight. "Where's the keys?"

"Fuck, dude. I don't know."

He punched me in the shoulder again, harder this time. "Well, you better find them, or I'm really gonna kick your ass!"

"Check my pants," I said, pointing to the chair they were draped on.

"No. You check your pants. It looks like you pissed them!"

I sat back down and reached into my pants pockets.

"Here they are," I said, handing them to him as I started to get back into bed.

"What do you think you're doing? Get up!" he said, pulling me back to my feet. "Show me where my car is. I'm late. Can you even remember where you parked it? Or is it in a gutter somewhere?"

"Yeah. I memebbr," I slurred. "I'll show you…It's on the lower lot at the bottom of campus along Alvarado Drive."

We left the condo and walked back west along Alvarado Drive toward the campus lot. By now he was fuming. Ten minutes later, we arrived at the lot. His brown 1976 Pinto hatchback was right where I said it was—along the back row of the lower lot. While unharmed, it looked like a turd on wheels. But it was a car—more than I had. My friend was kind enough to loan it to me, and I broke that trust by getting drunk and not giving it back to him before I passed out.

"See, I told you I knew where it was, and it's all intact."

"Well, it's a damn good thing. Otherwise, I'd really have to kick your ass!"

Broken

Reality hit me like a ton of bricks. I started to realize that I wasn't going to be able to get myself out of this on my own, even though I still wanted to try.

After my accident in San Diego that nearly cost me my right hand, I knew my alcoholism and drug addiction were completely out of control, and that I needed help. I decided to look up "alcoholism" in the phone book, and found a number for AA. I took a deep breath and dialed the number.

The person on the other end asked me a few questions and told me to go to a meeting, but I was scared, and never went.

Then I called my mom for advice, even though I already knew the right thing to do. She asked how I was doing. I tried to pretend that all was "fine," but then I cracked.

"I can handle it," I pretended.

"No. You have no job, no money, and you need to come home and get better. You don't get to vote. I'm getting you a plane ticket and you need to come home."

"But Mom, if I come home and quit school, I'll feel like I've failed—like I let you down…let myself down…. I can do this."

"No, Son. Sometimes you have to fall before you can get up again. It doesn't make you a failure. It means you need help. You need to get better. Let me help. You need to come home. Now."

"I don't want to be a failure." I was devastated. My pride was wounded and, as much as I had dreamt of going away to school and making it on my own, I had to accept the fact that I needed help.

"You chose to go to school," she said. " You can go back to school and finish. But you need to get better first. Come home." Her tone was firm. Even as assertive as she was being, I found comfort in her insistence.

"Ok. I guess I don't really have a choice," I sighed, conveying frustration even as I felt relief. I wanted so badly to be independent, now I had to go back to mom.

"I'll get you a plane ticket and send it to you."

"Thanks, Mom." I heard her sigh on the other end of the line.

While waiting for my ticket, I let my roommates know I was moving out. Then I started packing up my stuff. I'd have to leave some in storage. I had a chair, a couple lamps, a solid oak door that sat on sawhorses as my desk, a piece of crap stereo and cheap ass speakers along with some posters, books and other belongings that I couldn't take with me. It was all junk, yet seemed valuable enough to store in a $15/month storage locker. I packed up my clothes in a large duffle bag and got some twine to take my futon with me so I'd have a bed when I got to my mom's house. Then I called Duane to help me take my stuff to the storage facility. Once again, he came through.

The next day I tied up my futon and made a shoulder strap out of twine. That afternoon, I tossed my duffle and futon into my roommate's car and headed for the airport.

Traffic was light until we got a half mile from the airport where it came to a standstill. We were not moving at all and I started worrying that I would miss my flight.

"Don, I'm going to have to run if I want to make it in time."

"You can't," he said. "You have that big futon and a duffle bag to carry." I looked at my stuff in the backseat, my mind racing as I tried to figure out how this could work. I didn't see any other choice. "I have to," I told him. "If I don't, I'll miss my flight and I don't have any money to pay for a flight change."

"All right, hold on." There was no turnout lane, so he pulled onto the curb, parked, and then popped the hatchback. I slung my duffle bag over my left shoulder and my futon over my right, and then slammed the hatchback closed.

"Bye. Thank you!" I said, nodding my head without any hands free.

"Take care," he said, nodding back.

I took off running toward the Southwest gate. After three-hundred feet or so, I was dripping sweat. The bag and bed kept slapping the backs of my legs, causing me to stumble. I felt ridiculous sprinting down the road carrying my bed and luggage.

I made it to the check-in counter just in time. I found my gate, climbed aboard and was off. An hour and twenty minutes later, I was on the ground in Oakland.

Chapter 12
Home

My brother, Kelly and sister-in-law, Angel, picked me up and took me to my mom's new home in Fairfax. When we arrived from the airport, Angel showed me to my room.

"Here you go. Welcome home, bro!" she said, giving me a hug. "We made a platform for you, with sheets and a pillow." She turned on the lamp and showed me where I could hang my clothes. Then she left me to get situated.

It was a tiny 10'x8' room. The ceiling was low, and the double hung window opened to a view of the creek and the backside of the post office. I unfolded my futon, and tossed my duffle bag in the corner. There wasn't much room for anything else, but it would be my home while I figured out what to do next. I went upstairs and gave my mom a big hug and thanked her for bailing me out.

I had come home with the intent of controlling my drinking and getting my shit together, so the next day I started looking for work. I picked up a copy of the local newspaper, the Marin IJ, and saw an ad in the classified section, for a waiter at the Marin Steak House in San Anselmo. I went down to apply for the job and met the owner. He was a large Greek man with a great smile and huge moustache. He looked a little like Captain Kangaroo. I filled out an application and handed it to the owner. He looked it over and asked me a few questions about my work history.

Even though I still had a broken finger, he hired me on the spot. I would start the next day.

The uniform was supposed to be a suit or tuxedo. I was broke, so I borrowed $40 from my mom and found an oversized wool tuxedo and a bowtie at a local thrift store. It was way too big and heavy, but it would have to do. That summer was very hot, and with only a big fan to cool the dining room, it made me sweat like a pig. It was embarrassing, but I dealt with it.

The best part of waiting tables is the instant cash. I worked four to five nights a week and made enough tips for beer money and a little rent money for my mom.

A week or so after got the job, I called the surgeon in Los Angeles who referred me to an orthopedic surgeon in Marin, Dr. Hand. I thought he was kidding. I called and made an appointment. After the nurse took x-rays, and Dr. Hand looked over my hand, he told me it was healing well. We set an appointment in another two weeks to get the stainless steel pin removed from my right finger.

Two weeks later, I was back.

"Have a seat and Dr. Hook will be with you in a moment," the nurse said as she sat me in the exam room.

"Dr. Hook? I thought I was seeing Dr. Hand?" I asked trying to take this seriously.

"Oh, Dr. Hand is on vacation," she said. "His colleague, Dr. Hook is the specialist on duty today."

I felt like I was living in an episode of "The Twilight Zone."

I took a seat, and in walked Dr. Hook. He looked like Michael Douglas or Douglas Fairbanks—tall, handsome and tan, with slick black hair. He moved and spoke quickly. Flipping through my chart, he looked up and said, "So you had a wrestling match with a Pepsi machine and busted your finger?" He raised his thick eyebrows, a wry grin on his face.

"Yeah—not a good move," I answered, rolling my eyes.

"Well, we'll get that pin out," he promised.

Already a little uneasy that I was going to have a pin removed by a doctor named *Hook*, I asked, 'So, Dr. Hook, is that your real name?"

"Yep."

"How are you going to remove the pin?"

"Oh…" He paused while turning to open a cabinet. After fumbling around for a moment, he found his instrument.

"Pliers," he said, holding them up. "They work like a charm." I eyed the pliers warily, briefly considering keeping the pin in forever.

"Will it hurt?" I asked.

"Nah—piece of cake. Give me your hand." He pinched the end of the steel rod with the pliers, wiggled it a little, then, with a swift tug, pulled the stainless pin out.

I looked at my hand, wiggling my fingers. My index finger was stiff, but at least I could move it.

"That surgeon in San Diego did a good job," I said, looking at the hole where the pin was and feeling grateful that I didn't lose my finger.

"Yes, he did," Dr. Hook replied. "You were lucky. That hole should heal up in a couple days. Stay away from vending machines, okay?"

"Will do. Thanks, Doc."

My finger remained a little stiff for a few days, but in another week it was nearly as good as new.

The days and weeks at Marin Steak House seemed to fly by. I was making money and having fun. Our hostess, Gina, was a cute buxom redhead who was very flirty. It wasn't long before we hooked up, and once again I felt on top of the world as things started to fall in place.

My days all seemed to run together and became fairly routine. If I wasn't going home with Gina, I'd hit the bars and play pool, or listen to music. Most nights, I'd stay out partying until the early hours of the morning, and then stagger home and sleep until 3 p.m. before I had to go to work the next evening—not much different from my high school years working as a server at the Yacht Club, then as a busboy and valet at Dominic's in San Rafael before I went away to college. I made really good money and had little responsibility, then I literally pissed it all away. It was an easy, nowhere life.

My *routine* nearly always included beer—lots of beer. Sometimes I'd grab a twelve pack on the way home and drink with my brother and his friends. The living room in the downstairs "apartment" at my mom's house was a perfect party cave—there were no windows. On the weekends, we'd sometimes get coke and stay up all night tweaking while we played 5000 or Yahtzee. I don't remember a lot about what happened over the next several months, as my drinking got progressively worse. I was drinking myself into oblivion, blacking out, passing out, and seeking out lower companions at the local bars. I was partying all the time.

Three weeks earlier, I got so drunk at a local bar in San Anselmo that a couple friends from high school had to bring me home. All I remember was drinking a few "smoky martinis" that went straight to my head, and I didn't even like gin. I was lit in no time and I couldn't even hold myself up on the barstool. The bartender cut me off and 86'd me.

As I staggered toward the door, sure I could find my way home, Ernie, one of the friends I had been drinking with offered to help.

"You're not driving are you? You sure you can get home?"

"No, I'm walking. I got it," I said, full of drunken bravado before face planting on the sidewalk outside the bar.

There was something about that stretch of road. Five years earlier at seventeen, I had gotten wasted on tequila with James, the guy who first introduced himself when I moved to Woodacre. We were weaving our way down Sir Francis Drake toward the Hub. I had no business driving. I did my best to keep my mom's Ford Courier centered between the dotted lines as we swerved left and right. The Twin Cities police pulled us over. No need for a sobriety test then. We were wasted. I ran my mouth, slurring that I wasn't drunk. James told me to shut up. This was before there were harsher drunk driving laws.

"Where's home?" the cop asked. James told him that his dad's apartment was just down the street. The officer instructed us to park the car on San Anselmo Ave., and put us in the back of the cop car. He then drove to the Kentfield apartment. Grace showed her face once again.

Five years later, there I was on the same stretch of road, face down on the sidewalk in front of the bar. Ernie and another Drake alumni, Buck, came to my rescue.

"You're not going anywhere alone," Buck said, lifting me to my feet. "Where's home?"

"Fairfax…that way," I pointed to Kentfield, wobbling as I tried to stay upright.

"No, Fairfax is that way," Ernie said, spinning me toward Fairfax like a blindfolded kid at a birthday party, only there was no donkey to pin the tail on or piñata to hit. "Where in Fairfax?"

"Mmmmmono," I slurred. "By the movie theat…t…t… er."

"What's the address?" Buck asked, looking at me like I was a wounded dog.

"MMMono…. I'll show you…." I slurred.

"Come on, well get you home safe," Buck said, holding me up under the arm and nodding to Ernie to guide me by the other arm.

The next thing I remember I was opening the door to the downstairs apartment. We had just gotten two kittens. As I door opened, the kittens took off. Buck and Ernie somehow managed to track them down.

"All right, dude…sleep it off," Buck said, closing the door.

Safely inside, I started toward the back bedroom, staggered two steps, then passed out on the kitchen floor.

"Dude! Wake up! You need help!" Angel said, shaking me awake the following morning. She was right.

Chapter 13
Defining Moments

A month or so earlier, some of my brother's friends who had been staying with us for a bit had grown tired with all the partying and went to an AA meeting. They came home with a sense of hope and some AA literature—the twenty questions to determine if you are an alcoholic and a meeting schedule. I read through the twenty questions brochure and answered yes to several of them. Then I read the fine print at the bottom that said that if you answered yes to three or more of the twenty, chances are that you have a problem with drinking and could be an alcoholic.

Damn! I thought. I might, kind-of, sort-of, have a problem. But I wasn't ready to stop. *How would I have any fun without booze? How would I be social? How would I get out of my shell of fear and insecurity? What would I do to fill the hole—that aching hole in my heart?* I wasn't ready to give up booze. I wasn't fully convinced I had a problem. Even in those moments where my life was going to shit, I was still in denial, believing that I could control it on my own.

It's been said that alcoholism is a disease that tells you that you don't have a disease. In many respects, it's a disease of insanity. In fact, before AA, many alcoholics were locked up in insane asylums because the medical, psychological, and psychiatric community had little understanding of alcoholism, let alone an agreed upon method of treatment. Today, there are many choices for recovery. One solution can be found in the "Big Book," *Alcoholics Anonymous,* which outlines a 12-step program of recovery in the first 164 pages that has helped millions of alcoholics worldwide stop drinking when they followed and worked the 12-steps.

Hitting Bottom

One hot July night after my shift at the Marin Steak House, I staggered from bar to bar on a quest to get drunk and/or get laid—two things that don't always go hand in hand. After a few beers—liquid courage, I actually thought I my oversized thrift store suit looked smashing. How delusional! That night I would not "get lucky." Instead all I got was drunk and remorseful.

I drank until closing time, left the bars, and then wandered up Bolinas Avenue to Deer Park. I found a path leading toward the top of the ridge and walked around aimlessly for a while. It was pitch black. I was lost—figuratively and literally. I felt like my life was going nowhere. All I could hear was my shuffling footsteps and crickets as I meandered along the dark trail flanked by oaks and scrub brush.

After a bit, the trail opened up to a clearing. The dim glow of street lights beckoned in the distance, giving me a sense of direction. I staggered toward them, down a small hill covered with tall dry wheat like grass—the kind that looks like a golden ocean on a breezy summer day. It looked soft and inviting. I took two steps and realized it was slick with morning dew. I slipped and was rolling down the hill. Burrs and stickers covered my *fancy suit.* What a sorry sight!

I sat for a moment in the damp grass. *What was I doing? How did I get here? Why?* I wondered. *Why can't I control this? I had so much, and now I have nothing. What's the use?* Maudlin and despondent, tears streamed down my cheeks as thoughts of ending it all filled my hazy brain.

The first light of dawn made its way over the ridge. Rays filtered through the treetops. Then a thought jumped into my head, that today I can only call a miracle—*meeting—there's a meeting at 7 a.m., down the hill, at the Women's Center.*

That meeting schedule from a month ago was no accident. Somehow, in my despair, I recalled that there was a daily meeting at the Fairfax Women's Center at 7 a.m., not far from where I was.

The sun was just coming up. It had to be about 6-6:30 a.m. I could make it. I wiped my bloodshot eyes, stumbled to my feet, and did my best to pick the stickers out of my suit. Then I made my way toward town. I staggered along Bolinas Avenue to the 7-Eleven that was directly across the street from both the Women's Club and Fairfax Police Department.

Getting scared about what to expect—*Maybe I should get a beer first? Maybe I need to be drunk to be at a meeting? Who knows? If I'm going to give this a shot, I better have one last one.* I went into the store, bought two beers and chugged them in the parking lot before going to the meeting across the street.

The thought and decision to go to a meeting was another "God moment"—though I wouldn't know that until much later. Some things may be seen as merely coincidence; others may be perceived as divine intervention or inspiration, or whatever one chooses to believe. They are small miracles. Today I call these moments of temporary clarity "God's grace." Time and time again, when in the valley of despair or facing a tough decision I have found that I am always given a way out. It takes practice to look for it. It starts with prayer—asking for help.

This was one of those moments. The thought came into my head, and I made a decision to walk into my first AA meeting.

I could smell the coffee brewing. I had been up all night and smelled like a brewery. My tuxedo was still covered with burrs and stickers. I grabbed a cup of coffee and found a seat.

When the meeting began, the group said the "Serenity Prayer" aloud, then someone read the 12-steps and another read the 12-traditions. Throughout the reading of the steps and traditions I heard the word God and it scared me. I didn't know what to think. *It's a cult*, I thought.

Then they asked if any new members would like to stand and introduce themselves. One or two others announced their name and said they were an alcoholic. I had never said publicly that I was an alcoholic. I didn't know what one was. It was my turn. I stumbled to my feet, nearly spilling the hot coffee in my lap, and, following the others, boldly announced,

"My name is Shawn-n-imnnalcohoilc."

"Hi Shawn," the group said in unison, then applauded. I didn't know what any of the protocols were, but found it odd that I got applause for being an alcoholic.

A few people shared, but I don't remember anything that was said.

At the close of the meeting we all stood, held hands and recited the Lord's Prayer aloud. This was the first time I had ever heard it.

Afterward an old timer came up to greet me. "I'm Charlie," he said, shaking my hand.

He was a short, stocky man with a great smile, who reminded me of the character on the Chance cards in Monopoly. After listening to a brief bit of nonsense out of my mouth, he gave me his number and said to get a sponsor and call if I wanted a ride to a meeting.

"Yeah, I don't know about this God thing," I said. "I think I can do it on my own."

I don't recall his exact reply, but the gist of it was that he wasn't buying my bullshit—he said he'd been sober a while, and had heard it all before.

"You're not ready. You're not done drinking yet," Charlie said directly. I wish I could say that he was wrong. He wasn't. It took me another three months before I would truly be ready. I was still in fear; still in denial.

For any worthy endeavor, it requires courage to take the first step. I was still looking to the bottle for my courage. I wasn't done drinking yet. Charlie was right.

I left that meeting and went home agonizing over what I would do. *How could I let go of booze? It got me out of my shell.* When I was feeling inadequate it temporarily filled the hole inside. I wasn't afraid to talk to women as long as I had a few beers in me. I didn't have to face my feelings when I got drunk. Booze had become my best friend. I'd be bored to death without it. *How could I hang with my friends if I wasn't drinking?*

Like a machine gun, excuses of why I couldn't stop drinking raced through my mind at rapid fire.

I smoked a cigarette and passed out for a few hours before I had to go to work. When I woke up, I showered and left for work. The whole night I kept thinking about that number in my pants. When I was done with work I went home and didn't drink for a night. That was the first time in a long time. I was in agony. I smoked like a chimney instead.

The next day was lobster night at the Steak House— always a busy night. I made some good money, and decided to celebrate with a few beers. I came home and drank a little with my brother and his friends, but he had to get up early the next morning and went to bed. The night was young so I went to one of the bars in Fairfax. I ordered a vodka tonic and pounded it. Nothing. I then ordered a double. Still no buzz.

There comes a time for alcoholics where booze stops working. I had never experienced this before. I ordered another and finally accepted that I was not getting a buzz that night. I decided to go into the back and play some pool. I met a spunky blonde girl that was buzzed and a total flirt. We played pool for a bit. After she kicked my butt a few times, she asked me to take her home. It had been a while and, at twenty-two, I didn't think twice. We wandered down the alley behind the Fairfax Theater to my home at the end of the block. She, too, had been celibate a while, and that night we made up for our sexual droughts.

We finally fell asleep as the sun was coming up. When I awoke, she was gone, but had left a poem on my nightstand next to my overflowing ashtray. I don't recall the whole thing except for one verse that has stuck with me all these years— "...Let innocence be your stepping stone..."

Something in those words struck me. Though I was a twenty-two-year-old drunk, she must have seen some spark inside me in our brief time together, some ray of hope— innocence, as she called it—that inspired her to leave me a poem. I never saw her again.

I was getting bored with the Marin Steak House. I saw in the classifieds that The Lark Creek Inn was hiring. This was a dream restaurant; I had wanted to work there so bad before I left for college, but was in a great spot at Dominic's. I went by, filled out an application, and was hired on the spot.

The restaurant was a quaint converted Victorian home that sat along a tree lined creek in Larkspur.

This was fine dining and required a higher level of attentiveness and service than most restaurants. I had done well as a valet and busboy at Dominic's all through high school, but now my drinking was affecting my ability to remember table numbers and orders like I used to. For training, I was given a small section of three to four tables to work during lunch service. The first two days of training went well, but there was a lot to remember. Plus, lunch service required a much faster pace than I was used to. I handled it, and, on the third day of training I was given the chance to serve a small wedding reception for brunch in the upstairs banquet room.

As I approached the table, I recognized one of the guests from my high school days. He was a construction worker who often picked me up hitchhiking on my way to school, usually when he had beer between his legs. Now, he wasn't drinking. Neither was the bride and groom, or anyone else in the party. Yet, they were laughing and having a good time. It seemed odd.

On subsequent shifts, I could barely remember the table numbers. I'd forget orders, and was just lost. Sadly, my brain was too wet to handle the high volume and level of service needed to work at the Lark Creek Inn.

One day, several of us were scheduled to work split shifts. In between shifts, a small group of us went down the street to the infamous Silver Peso in Larkspur. In no time, I was so hammered I couldn't even sit up on the bar stool, so I passed out on the sofa in the corner.

I don't know how long I was out for, but was awakened by the bartender who said my manager was on the phone. The bartender handed me the phone.

"You're late. You better get up here," my manager barked through the phone.

"I'm sorry. I don't think I can work tonight," I apologized. Looking around, I noticed that my co-workers had already left.

"Have you been drinking?" *Well, duh, you don't go to a bar just to play shuffleboard,* I thought.

"Yeah…a little," I slurred.

"Well, we need you now," he coaxed me, tying to be understanding.

"I'm sorry, I can't work tonight…. I'm too drunk-n-thatsjustthewayitis…."

"Then, you're fired!" He hung up the phone.

Years later, I went back to the Lark Creek Inn and was rehired. I was ready, and in a year, learned more about the art of fine dining than the previous fifteen combined. It was fun, and the money was enough to pay the bills.

Voices

Have you ever been so drunk that you got the spins—when you feel like you're on the Round-up or Tilt-a-Whirl ride at a county fair, only this ride is not any fun? You dangle one foot off the bed in a vain effort to make it stop. Sometimes it helps, other times, just like the Tilt-a-Whirl after a couple corn dogs, you want to puke.

How about dropping acid and being certain that someone picked up the house and turned it 180 degrees? What about blackouts or auditory and visual hallucinations? Have you ever been so high that you hear voices? I was there.

Sometime between that first meeting in July and October of 1986, my drinking and drug use had escalated to the point where I needed to drink or use drugs every single day just to cope. No matter how much I tried to control it, I had no power over its deadly grip.

I had been able to stop drinking for brief periods, usually no more than three or four days in a row, but was still doing cocaine and acid. Talk about being crazier than a shithouse rat—like a lemming, I was headed for the cliff fast.

On sheer will power, I managed to stop drinking for four days, but still thought about drinking all the time. One night, after work I came home to my brother and his friends drinking shots of tequila. It smelled good. The urge was awakened. I needed a drink. The compulsion won. I grabbed the bottle, chugged three big gulps, and I was off to the races again. The next few months were mostly a blur.

Later that summer, after lots of drugs and drinking, I staggered home to my "cave" of a room. I was so depressed, and, honestly, I didn't know why. I plopped onto the bed and stared at the low wainscot ceiling. My head was swimming. My heart was racing so fast that I felt I had to consciously focus on my breathing or I'd die.

I couldn't go to sleep. Panic set in. I focused on the beaded cracks in the wainscot ceiling six feet above my head. I found cracks in the paint—imperfections. My mind wandered and my breathing steadied. I closed my eyes briefly. The brief silence was quickly erased by hallucinations and voices. In a rush, I saw images of everyone I ever knew. It was so vivid. Faces of my mom, my dad, my brothers, my grandparents, my aunts and uncles, close friends, loved ones, childhood friends…anyone and everyone I had ever crossed paths with paid me a visit. They all said the same thing—*"We love you—get help."*

It was as if they were in my head. I thought I was losing my mind—going crazy. Either that, or I was dying. I wept. I was too afraid to die. Maybe it was the booze, or the drugs. I sobbed out loud, and cried out for help, *God, please help me. I'm scared and I don't know what is going on. Either I'm going crazy, or I'm going to die or it's the drugs and booze. Please, dear God, help me! I don't know what to do. Give me a sign. Help me out of this, I don't want to die!* In that moment of complete and utter defeat my room filled with light.

The images of all those who loved me smiled and rejoiced in my surrender.

"You will be okay," they said in a chorus. *"Let it go—get help."*

In that moment, I felt protected. No matter what I had done to get there, I suddenly knew there was a way out. There was hope.

So began the next phase of my journey to sincerely seek help and recovery.

I wish I could say that the flash of light came down upon me like a bolt of lightning, and that I was instantly "cured." Life doesn't usually work like that. Most success in life requires repeated failure and willingness to get back up and try again. It has also been my experience that of ourselves we are nothing. We need support from others, and some sort of faith and belief in something greater than us. What's more, virtually any successful endeavor requires effort; that four-letter word—*work*. In other words—faith without works is dead.

It would take a couple more runs to finally get me to the place of sincerely becoming willing to let go of my "best friend," booze.

One Sunday afternoon, I awoke to my mother's voice upstairs. It sounded like she was on the phone.

"Yes, he's not himself," I heard her say. "I am at my wits end and don't know what to do. He can't stop drinking and using drugs. He's crazy. He stays out all night, sleeps all day and is killing himself with drugs and alcohol." There was a pause, then she said, "So when can you come by? Will you put him in a strait jacket?"

The conversation freaked me out. My mind raced, thinking of being hauled away to an insane asylum. I stared out the double hung window that overlooked the creek behind the Fairfax Post Office. I saw nothing. My mind was a thousand miles away. *I better make a run for it*, I thought, and I began to climb out the window wearing nothing but my white briefs. The thought entered my head that I should go talk to my mom. I stopped, and pulled myself back into my room. Then I walked up the back stairs, across the rickety deck, and through both sets of French doors to where she sat in the living room over my room.

"What's the matter, honey?" she asked. She gave me a curious look as I stood in front of her wearing nothing but my underwear.

"I heard you on the phone, talking to the insane asylum. Are they coming to take me away?"

"Oh honey," she sighed. She gave me a sad look. "No. I wasn't on the phone. Nobody is coming to take you away." She opened her arms. "Come here," she said. Something inside me broke. I went to her and she folded me inside her embrace, holding me as she'd done countless times before when I was a child.

I broke down, unable to contain the stress that had been mounting since before I came home in April.

"Oh sweetie, you need to get help," she said as I cried. "No, I am not having you committed. There's no white wagon on the way—no strait jackets." She let me cry a little longer, stroking my hair. I was too far gone to feel silly, a grown man folded into his mother's lap, weeping.

"Go put some clothes on and I'll make you a sandwich," she said.

A mother's love is enough—enough to cut though any hurt, any pain. My mom helped to get me back on my feet.

A week or so later, I awoke to a gift that would be the catalyst to change my life. Next to my overflowing ashtray was a card from my mom. On the face of the card was an image of fifty or more penguins standing on an iceberg. In the center was one lone sun-burnt penguin who stood out like a sore thumb.

Inside she had written:

> *Son,*
>
> *You are one in a million! I love you too much to watch you slowly die. Please get help! I love you!*
>
> *Love,*
>
> *Mom*

More than a simple gesture, it was really a last ditch effort to save me. My alcohol and drug abuse had only gotten worse since I came home. That day, in September of 1986, she threw me a lifeline.

That card represented the love, compassion and care of a mother who was watching her twenty-two-year-old son slowly kill himself. It cut through the thick veil of my pain and denial, and grabbed me by the heart strings. It made me take pause. However, I didn't immediately seek help. I read that card many times over the next several weeks—usually in a drunken stupor when I was feeling lost and all alone. My mother's love expressed in a mere greeting card was the miracle that got me back on track and set me on the path to a life I never imagined. It was one of several catalysts that changed my life.

Made a Decision

October 9, 1986, I had just finished having dinner with my mom when there was a knock on the door. Three of my longtime friends—James, Joe, and Scott—stood at the top of the steps.

"Langwell. What's up?" Scott announced, grinning. "We're going to listen to reggae music and party. Wanna go?"

Earlier that afternoon I had made a decision to go into rehab. I was going to quit it all for good, and my conviction was already being tested.

"Hey guys. I'd love to, but I'm done partying. I need to go into rehab," I said, feeling ashamed.

"What? You aren't that bad. C'mon, you don't need to party, we can just listen to music," James coaxed.

My mind was made up. "Thanks, but I know how I get when I party, and it's probably not a good idea. Have fun." I looked away, not wanting to change my mind.

"Hey, good for you," Joe said, with a serious look. He knew.

"Take care," James said. "Love ya."

"Thanks guys. This is a tough decision, but its time. We'll still be friends. I just need to get some help right now."

My mind reeled with thoughts of whether I actually would lose my friends over this. As the guys left, I wondered if I'd ever be able to have any fun again. Inside, I knew this was the right thing to do—my life depended on it.

Earlier that afternoon, I had grabbed the phone book and made several calls to rehab facilities. I found that Ross Hospital had a twenty-eight day recovery program in Kentfield. Ironically, it was three blocks from where James and I used to party at his dad's apartment. I would be going in the next evening.

I packed a duffle bag with clothes and basic sundries. The next day, when Kelly came home from work, we had a quick dinner and he drove me to the hospital to check in. We barely spoke on the ride over. He pulled his 1967 white Chevy truck into the lot and parked.

"You sure you want to do this?" he asked.

"Yes. I've made up my mind." And I had. I knew there was no other choice. I was done killing myself.

"Okay, let's go," Kelly said.

I grabbed my bag and he walked me to the door. I paused just outside to give him a hug goodbye. For a split second I had second thoughts. I shook it off, arming myself with determination.

"Love you, bro," I said holding onto him longer than normal.

"I love you, too. Get better," he said, returning the embrace, squeezing me tight before letting me go.

I turned and stepped across the threshold. And I never looked back.

Chapter 14
Recovery

I took the elevator up to the third floor and checked in. I would be required to detox in a private room under twenty-four hour supervision for the first seventy-two hours. I would have no contact with the outside world for the first week. It sucked having to sit in a room with no booze, no TV, no distractions, and very little human contact. The only interaction I had was with the nurse and doctor making rounds every three to four hours. I was locked in the virtual solitary confinement of my own brain for the three full days—a dangerous place to be alone, but I made it through. I slept a lot and, after the second day, started to feel better. I wanted to be let into the general population of the twenty-eight day recovery facility after the second day—hey, I was cured, I could handle it, right?—wrong. The nursing staff had to follow protocol, and insisted I stay put, no exceptions.

Over the next twenty-five days, I would learn about the insidiousness of alcoholism—that it is a disease that tells you that you don't have a problem—that it's a mental obsession of the mind (craving) coupled with a physical allergy to alcohol and other mind altering chemicals. I would be introduced to the 12-steps of AA. There were fifteen or so others going through rehab at the time I was there. We met with counselors to learn more about the steps and work through exercises to unravel some of the underlying issues behind our addictions.

There were also meetings. At first they were solely on site, then there were excursions to other meetings in the area after the first two weeks. One thing that struck me early on was the fear they put in me. The recovery rate for long term sobriety is relatively low, they said—only one out of three stay clean and sober for ten or more years. Not because the program doesn't work, but because most addicts don't work the program. Like anything worthwhile in life, recovery takes effort. As my good friend, Antony, will attest, if someone tells me that I can't do something, I will put one hundred ten percent effort into proving them wrong as long as it's healthy, legal and ethical. Hearing the low stats was enough fuel for me to fully commit to getting clean and sober. Self-will helped me stay sober in the beginning, but in the months to follow, I would realize that sobriety requires addicts and alcoholics to find a "power greater than ourselves" to help us stay sober.

The word *God* scared me away from that very first meeting I went to in Fairfax. But, now, I had no other options. I surrendered one hundred percent to the program of recovery.

Sunday nights were family nights, and the old timer who had told me I wasn't ready months earlier was there. Remembering me from the morning meeting, he smiled. Another coincidence? I was beginning to think not.

Two weeks or so into rehab, the counselors suggested that I look into Marin Services for Men (MSM) for transitional housing when I got out. I called the director, Jennifer, and introduced myself. She politely said that she would put me on a waiting list.

"How far down am I?" I asked.

"You're at the bottom of the list. There are twenty people ahead of you," she said bluntly. My heart sank. If I went back to the apartment with my brother and sister-in-law, I knew I was going to drink again.

"What do I have to do to get to the top of the list and get in?" I was determined to do whatever it took.

"Call me every day for the next week," she replied, unemotionally as if she'd had this conversation many times before. She probably had.

And, so I did. I called every single day for a week. I breathed a huge sigh of relief when, on the last day before release, she let me know I had been accepted.

When I went into the twenty-eight day program, I had nothing. No material possessions. No work. When I left, all I had was twenty-eight days of recovery, a growing faith, and a determination to succeed. That was enough. I was willing to go to any lengths to stay sober, but I needed a higher power to help me. As I worked the steps with a sponsor, I would find and nurture my spiritual connection to a power greater than myself that would evolve in the days, weeks, months and years to follow.

Trusting God to help me recover was not something that happened overnight. It took a lot of soul searching and step work, as well as leveling my pride to completely let go. All I needed in the beginning was willingness and humility. I had made several half-hearted attempts to stop on my own. Now I was on my way with the help of God and a sponsor to guide me through the 12 steps. I was beginning to believe I could make it.

Immediately after moving into Marin Services for Men (MSM), my roommate, Ed, who was a plumbing contractor, put me to work. I made $15 per hour, which was enough to cover my rent and have some left over for spending money. A week or so later we got another roommate, Melton, who would also work with us and become a great friend.

Shortly thereafter, I heard there was a new Mexican restaurant opening in Terra Linda where the old Velvet Turtle was. It was called Casa Carlita's. I applied and was hired immediately.

It was a good job for a while. I was nervous at first to be back in the restaurant business serving alcohol especially when many younger people I worked with loved to party. But I was determined to make it work, I was attending classes during the day at College of Marin, working nights at the restaurant, and continuing to work my steps. Things were finally starting to fall into place.

With my new job, a few bucks in my pocket, and six months of recovery, I was feeling good and got a bit cocky. To add to the chaos, I was sleeping with someone at work, but later found out that I wasn't the only one who was sleeping with her. I was walking a slippery slope, it's a wonder I stayed sober.

Even though I was only there a short time, I wasn't happy at the Mexican restaurant. Fortunately, I heard about a new Italian Restaurant opening in downtown San Rafael. I applied for it, and got the job. I would be starting in two weeks.

As an experienced server in higher-end restaurants, I took my job seriously and always strived to be attentive, cordial, efficient, and entertaining for my customers. I was accustomed to more expensive restaurants, which meant better tips. This place was a serious step down, and I got an attitude about it. But I needed money.

The dining room was huge with over fifty tables. The best tables lined a wall of windows each with a view of Mount Tamalpais. One Saturday night the restaurant was packed and we were running a forty-five minute wait. By the time people were seated, they were hungry and a little uptight. That said, the manager wanted us to "turn and burn" the tables, which is restaurant slang for serve the customers quickly and efficiently, without appearing to rush them, so they would eat, pay and leave. Then we could serve the next wave of customers. Typically, the more customers you served, the more you would make in tips.

Because this was an inexpensive restaurant, I had to wait on a lot of tables to make money. At the Marin Steak House, I made at least $100-$150 in tips per shift. At this place, it was more like $75-$85 on a good night.

The shift started out well, until two couples sat in my section at one of the nice window tables. I introduced myself and offered them margaritas. One said yes. The other three were still deciding. I returned to serve the one guest, then offered drinks to the other guests. Two of them ordered a margarita, as well, but the fourth customer was silent. I politely asked if he would like one, too.

"Perhaps a top-shelf one with Grand Marnier and Patron?" I suggested.

He didn't respond. He was a big guy and had a scowl on his face. He looked like he needed a drink, so I asked again. No look, no acknowledgement or anything. I walked away and returned a few minutes later with the other two margaritas.

"Where's mine?" the burly man with a ripped softball kisser asked.

"I'm sorry, I asked and you didn't respond. Would you like one as well?" I asked, biting my lip and trying to no show how irritated he was making me.

"Well, yeah, and I'm hungry, too. Can we order?" he demanded.

"Absolutely," I smiled, grabbing my pen and notepad to take their order.

"Aren't you going to get my drink?" the burly man glared at me, completely clueless that he just asked me to take their order. By now my patience was wearing thin.

"Certainly, I'll get it now." Looking for help from the other guests, hoping they could read my mind…. *Is this poor schmuck always so rude?* I flashed a fake smile, "Please excuse me, I'll be right back to take your order after I get his drink."

There was no attitude. Just trying to be professional. The rest of their time was like that. One drink, then another, then one who didn't want one, changed their mind. I must have made fifteen trips to the table. When they were done eating, I presented the check and came back to get change. They said to "keep it." The bill was $65 and inside was a fifty and a twenty—not even a ten-percent tip.

These people had busted my balls all night long. They had giggled each time I returned, making it seem like they were having me run back and forth, one drink at a time, on purpose.

As politely as possible, I asked if everything was to their liking.

"Why do you ask?" the gruff one said.

"Because I felt like I gave good service, but it wasn't reflected in the gratuity."

By the way, this is a cardinal sin for food servers. It's like a manager in baseball questioning an umpire about balls and strikes—you just don't do it.

"As a matter of fact," he continued, jutting his jaw out like a tough guy, "I don't like your attitude. You gave us crappy service and didn't even bring me my drink when I ordered it."

That was the last straw, my blood was boiling. I crossed the line as a professional server and did something I am not proud of—though, I imagine anyone who has been in the restaurant business for more than five years has thought about doing this.

"*My* attitude?! What about *yours*? You were having me run back and forth all night long, getting one drink at time 'cuz you thought it was funny to bust my chops on a busy night."

I raised my voice. Some diners turned to see what was going on. Over the years, I took great pride in my service and would do all I could to be attentive to my customers to make sure they were happy. This was a lost cause on these customers, they wouldn't know good service if it hit them in the face. They were entitled.

"Yeah, just like that. Your attitude sucks!" the big guy said as he stood and puffed his chest out. I clenched my jaw. If I was bigger I probably would've taken a swing.

"I'm sorry you feel that way. Really, I think you're the one with the shitty attitude," I said, raising my voice. By now everyone in the restaurant was watching this unfold. I took it to another level—

"Why don't you and your guests get the FUCK outta my restaurant, and take your shitty tip with you! YOU obviously need it more than I do!" Then I walked away.

The manager did his best to apologize to the guests for my outburst. Then he called me into his office. He asked for my side of the story. I told him. Then he said "I can't let you work here anymore. You're fired." I handed him my apron and left.

That was my last day working in a Mexican restaurant. Two days later, I was working at a local Italian restaurant where I would put myself through school, make great friends, and be on my way to making it on my own.

I felt bad about my outburst, but was glad to be working somewhere else. I realized that I still had a lot of internal work to do to exorcise my inner demons. Sure, alcohol was gone, but the dragons of past resentments and their twin sisters, pride and self-centered fear, began to rear their ugly heads. I had not yet developed a strong enough sense of serenity, and I let people and situations get to me. I snapped at the restaurant and was lucky I didn't drink over it.

I continued to work the steps and do what was suggested. In addition, at my sponsor's suggestion, I sought outside help and started seeing a therapist once a week for the next five years. My attitude began to change, my self-esteem improved. The chip on my shoulder began to disappear. I began to feel grateful and developed a sense of serenity and inner peace.

My life was getting better. I had been at Marin Services for Men for seven months and, with eight months of sobriety, felt confident and ready to "spread my wings." Melton and I decided to move in together and found a spacious apartment in the Canal area of San Rafael. That would be our home for the next five years.

Shortly after moving into our new apartment, I was accepted to San Francisco State University, and would start that fall. In the meantime, I was taking statistics at College of Marin over the summer.

Chapter 15
A Test of Faith

I never really connected with Grandma and Grandpa Snyder—at least not in the same way I did with my grandparents on my dad's side. As a result, my memories of them are just a few scattered pictures sprinkled with a story or two.

In my early teens Grandma Snyder, drove a classic white 1967 Chevelle that she had bought brand new. It was white with a red leather interior and hauled ass! It reeked of cigarette smoke, but I didn't care. I wanted that car so bad! My brothers and I were always impressed with how much power it had.

One day, my mom, Kelly, Seth, and I were on the way to a holiday party at my Great-Aunt Thelma's in San Jose. Grandma got a serious look on her face. Looking over her shoulder for oncoming traffic she floored it, pushing our backs deep into the red leather seats as she merged onto Highway 101 in Belmont. At first, this startled me. But on future visits, my brothers and I egged her on and couldn't wait to go for a ride with her. "Punch it Grandma!" we'd shout, and laugh our butts off as she flew down the 101.

My grandfather, Aaron Snyder was full blooded German who, like my grandma, smoked like a chimney. He was one of six children whose grandfather was part of the Jesse James gang.

We only visited around the holidays, so I never really knew him. The few memories I have of him were not necessarily warm and fuzzy. On family visits, Grandpa Snyder was always in his green patent leather La-Z-Boy recliner, smoking, coughing, and watching the fights or football. He couldn't quit; he continued to smoke even after he was diagnosed with emphysema.

"I'll be gone soon," he'd say while pulling away his oxygen mask to take a deep drag before hacking a lung. I can still hear the rattling in his chest as he coughed up the gunk from years of smoking. Emphysema inevitably took his life. I remember my mom also smoking every night after dinner, as well as my other grandparents who would hang out with their friends and relatives playing cards and drinking, laughing, and smoking. *I'll never smoke,* I had thought back then. I hated it. Well, that changed when I was away at school in San Diego. I dated someone who smoked and picked up that nasty habit. Some say it's more addictive than heroin. Fortunately I quit in 2012.

According to my mom, Grandpa Snyder liked to carry a silver flask filled with brandy to "keep the cold out" on brisk mornings while he repaired trains. She also said that he would often sneak out to the garage for a nip or two off a whiskey bottle stashed in his toolbox. Grandma didn't want him drinking in the house—beer was okay, but not the hard stuff.

When we visited, often the first thing my brothers and I did after saying hi and giving grandma a hug and a kiss was to make a beeline for the glass candy jar on their mantle. It was filled with Brach's peppermint candies—the round swirly kind you get at some restaurants and the soft 'chalky' mints that I still think are nasty. I only ate those after the others were gone. Inevitably, we'd eat most of the jar, only to later get yelled at by someone—either my mom, dad, or grandpa for eating too much candy.

All sugared up, Kelly and I would head outside to their backyard; Seth was too young and stayed inside with my mom and dad. It was a good sized yard with a large willow tree that offered some shade, and several healthy rose bushes that lined the back of their avocado green 1950s home. It was the home that my mom and her brother and sister grew up in. Like my dad's parents, Grandma and Grandpa Snyder lived in a generation where a family of five could easily afford a home and have a pension. They both worked and lived a comfortable life.

In the backyard, we headed straight to the white trunk. Inside were aluminum folding chairs, an old backyard badminton set, and various balls: a red bouncy ball, a volley ball, and an old weathered basketball that could've been the one my grandpa used in high school. Kelly and I would start a game of kickball in the backyard. On future visits, we'd throw the bouncy ball on the roof, then the basketball. We tossed it up and would race to catch it as it rolled off, sometimes right into grandma's roses. It must've been loud inside each time the ball hit the roof because my dad came out to scold us. He suggested we switched to a "lighter" ball. So we found an old tennis ball. Well, that was too light and would fly over the roof.

We'd race in through the kitchen door, past my parents and grandparents sitting in the living room to recover the ball that was now in the street.

"You better stop those kids, Jim!" my grandpa said as we flew out the front door, slamming it behind us. "That's a busy street and they could get hurt. Don't slam the door!" He barked.

So my dad would come tell us to go to the backyard and stay off the street and be safe. He handed us the ball as we went back out to continue our game.

We played for a bit more until the next time we threw the ball too far. We repeated the search, only this time it wasn't in the street. It had landed on the flat part of the roof that covered the front porch. So we did what any six or eight-year-old boy would do—we climbed onto the roof.

Hearing our footsteps thumping overhead, my grandpa was pissed, "Jim you better get those damn kids off the roof!"

I don't remember what ensued, but Kelly and I were in trouble. My dad was mad, my grandpa was mad. My dad spanked us and sent us to the spare bedroom. I could hear my mom, dad, and grandpa arguing in the living room. My grandma was in the kitchen cleaning up after dinner. I don't remember exactly what was said, but my mom later told me that he was an angry man when he drank and that she caught the brunt of his verbal rage as a kid. She could never say anything, neither could my grandmother. I never did see my grandmother and grandfather fight. Then again I never really saw them show affection for each other.

Well, after hearing my grandfather yell at us, my mom had enough. She finally had the courage to confront him, "You can't treat my kids the way you treated me!"

Later, my mom told me that my grandpa never really got over his youth. He drank and smoked because he couldn't deal with the pain of his childhood. In her mid-thirties he told her a story that put it all into proper perspective—one night his dad called four of the six children in their teens and early twenties to the kitchen table. He kissed each one on the forehead, then, without another word, went to the back bedroom, closed the door, and shot himself in the head.

I cannot even imagine what it would be like to live through that kind of trauma. How do you deal with it? The bottle was his way.

After Grandpa Snyder shared this story with my mom many years later, she had a different level of compassion for her father—she understood him and his pain. From that point forward she said, their relationship was incredible.

One evening in my late teens, the phone rang. I was in the living room at our Woodacre home, watching TV. My mom answered the phone. It was her mom, on the line.

"Oh, Pappa!" she howled, rocking herself as if her mother was holding her. "Oh Momma, no, not my daddy," she cried out to her mom on the other end of the phone, continuing to rock back and forth, tears streaming down her face.

I got up from the couch and went to the kitchen to comfort my mom, hugging her while she wept into the phone. She said goodbye to my grandma and hung up the phone, then she wrapped her arms around me continuing to grieve. I did my best to console her.

Back to School

One day, shortly after I had settled into my new apartment, I got a call from my mom on my way out the door to class.

"Hi honey, it's your mother." She always greets me this way as if I wouldn't recognize her voice. "Your grandmother isn't doing so well. She had to go to the hospital again last Tuesday."

"Which grandma?" I asked, looking at the clock. I had to catch the bus in ten minutes.

"My mom. Grandma Snyder," she said.

"Go back again? What do you mean?" I asked. I hadn't even known she was in the hospital before. "What happened?"

"She was really sick. They thought it was pneumonia." I could hear the concern in her voice. "Now she's got a staph infection. They say it doesn't look good." Her voice wavered, as she tried to be strong. "You may want to stop by and visit. I know you're not really close to her, but I'm sure she'd like to see you."

"I'm on my way to class right now, but I could stop by after. Where is she?" I asked, rushing the conversation as I looked at the clock.

"Marin General," my mom answered. "When does your class get out?"

"1:30. I'll stop by after." My mind raced, juggling my school schedule and my concern for my grandma. "What room, do you know?"

"No. Just ask the front desk when you get there."

"Okay. Bye. I gotta go or I'll miss my bus. Love you, Mom."

"I love you too, Son."

I grabbed my backpack and headed for the bus stop to go to my class. I choked down a carne asada burrito and a Camel cigarette on my way to class. Ever since the call with my mom, I kept thinking of my grandmother.

I recall visiting my grandmother in high school after she had sold her Belmont home and moved to an apartment in Fairfax to be closer to my mom. She was always so cordial. I'd sit in the chair next to her. A Bible sat on an end table between us, next to a large crystal ashtray overflowing with cigarette butts—she smoked Tareyton 100s like a chimney, and had really bad rheumatoid arthritis.

She offered me a Danish and a cup of coffee. And we sat and chatted for a bit. I told her about my plans to go to college, and work, and asked her how she was enjoying her new apartment—small talk. Really, my real purpose for visiting was to borrow her car. As I thought about it, I realized how selfish I had been. Now she was in the hospital and not doing well.

My stats class went by quickly. As soon as it was over I walked the mile and a half or so down Sir Francis Drake to visit my grandmother at Marin General Hospital. I entered the main lobby and approached the information kiosk where I was greeted by a sweet older woman.

"How may I help you young man?" she asked, smiling at me with kind eyes.

"I'm here to visit my grandmother, Henrietta Snyder," I announced, noticing her name badge said Madge. "Can you direct me to her room?"

"Sure, one moment," Madge said, flipping through the paper registry on her desk. "Snyder, you said?" she asked, raising her pencil thin eyebrows above her thick-rimmed glasses as she searched for my grandma's name.

"Yes—Henrietta," I said.

"Oh…" she sighed, rolling her eyes. "She's just been moved to ICU on the second floor." I felt like I had the wind knocked out of me. *Had I heard her right?*

"ICU?" I asked. *Please be wrong.*

"Yes—Intensive Care," she looked at me studying my face. "Are you a relative?" she asked.

"Yes. Her grandson, Shawn," I said, my mind reeling with a hundred what ifs. "Intensive care can't be good. Is she okay?"

"We don't have that information here," she said, her brow furrowing for a moment before she looked back at me. "Let me check with the duty nurse to see if she can have visitors." Starting to get worried, I felt my throat tighten. I could only nod. Madge picked up the phone talked for a few seconds before finally getting clearance.

"Elevator's over there," she said, pointing down the hall. She smiled, the worry gone from her face. "I'm glad you're here to visit," she told me.

I took the elevator up to the second floor. The doors opened right into the hall of the ICU. I could hear monitors chirping. A nurse scurried in the back corner. She moved with urgency. My heart rate skyrocketed.

I walked toward the nurses' station where a couple nurses gathered.

"Hi, I'm Shawn Langwell." I introduced myself to one of the nurses, who looked to be in charge. "I'm here to see Mrs. Snyder. I'm her grandson." He face took looked serious, she extended her hand.

"I'm Rene," she said, shaking my hand and looking me straight in the eyes. "Your grandmother has taken a turn for the worse. She's slipped into a coma," she said, leading me to my grandmother's room.

"Oh my God! What's wrong with her?" I asked, feeling my stomach tighten as I glanced toward my grandmother's motionless body. She had tubes in her nose for oxygen, and several leads running from her body to machines that monitored her vitals. Panic began to set in. I didn't want to be here alone if she died.

"She's got a really bad staph infection," Rene said, looking at my grandmother's chart. "Her body is trying to fight it off, but I have to be honest, it doesn't look good." She said, with an apologetic look.

At a loss for words, I bit my lip. I wasn't prepared for this. *What do I do?*

Sensing my fear and apprehension, Rene encouraged me to talk to my grandma, "She can still hear you even though she's in a coma," I grimaced, holding my breath.

"Well that's good, but I don't know what to say," I replied, looking at the floor. I was never that close and now I was with her all alone, my voice could be the last she hears before she dies, and I had nothing to say. This was all too overwhelming.

"Just tell her a story. Tell her you love her," Rene suggested, tilting her head and pursing her lips with an empathetic frown.

"I guess I can do that," I replied, with a half-hearted smile, feeling somewhat defeated. I wrestled with my feelings of care, compassion, and apathy. The real reason I was finding it so hard to come up with anything to say was because I barely knew my grandma. I loved her because she was family, but I had never felt any deep connection to her. I felt guilty because I had no deep remorse. Ironically, I was the only family member with her as she was nearing the end of her life.

My grandmother looked so frail. I was overcome with anxiety. I had no words. My mind raced. I knew I had to call my mom, but I needed a smoke first. I had to sort this out. I asked the nurse where the smoking area was, and she pointed to a door on the other side of the elevator.

I made my way to the balcony and lit up. The nicotine rush felt good. It helped me regain my composure before calling my mom. I choked down another and looked to the sky. Prayer was still new to me, but after eight months, of sobriety I had learned some basic prayers. This was different, though. I didn't know what to say, but somehow the words came to me.

Why God?! Why me? Why do I have to deal with this all alone? I am not ready for this! God, please, give me the courage and strength to not drink over this. Then, I said the "Serenity Prayer" out loud.

My emotions came crashing down on me. I sat for a minute, sobbing. When I had regained my composure I stood, wiped the tears away, then went back inside to call my mom.

I asked one of the nurses for permission to use their phone and called my mom at work. Fortunately, she answered. Doing my best to keep it together, I was direct and to the point. I brought her up to speed that grandma was not doing so good and that she needed to get here as soon as possible. She sighed and tried to hold back her tears, but inevitably, the tears won. She said she needed to get my brothers and call Uncle Gene and that she would be there as quick as possible.

I hung up and went to my grandmothers bedside.

"I love you, Grandma," I said, and then I leaned over to kiss her cheek. Her skin was cool under my lips.

The EKG monitor beeped loudly, scaring the crap outta me. I looked up at the monitor that emitted a high pitch uninterrupted single tone. She had flat lined.

"No! Grandma hold on," I cried out. "You can't go yet. My mom, isn't here yet—you know how much she'd want to say goodbye." I squeezed her hand begging for her to come back.

Rene rushed in to assess the situation. She checked the leads to make sure they were not pinched.

Oddly, I don't recall the nurse calling for a crash cart or anything. I remembered that Rene said my grandma could hear me, even though she couldn't respond. I was desperate. I was alone.

"Grandma, please come back," I pleaded, as tears streamed down my face. Beep. Beep. Beep. The EKG monitor chirped and showed her pulse. Miraculously, it was rising 50..65...82...*Whew*, I thought to myself. *Now what do I do?* I continued to talk to her. I told her that I loved her. I told her how cool it was that she drove her Chevelle fast. I apologized for not wanting to go to her husband's funeral, all while holding her arthritic hand. She looked so vacant. But I knew she knew I was there; even though she couldn't talk, I felt like she could still hear me. So I continued making peace.

I apologized for not spending more time with her. I told her again that she was a good Grandma with a good heart.

BEEEEEP. Flat lined again...

Fuck! I thought to myself, *I can't deal with this.* "Grandma, I know you are strong. And we both know how much it would mean for my mom and Gene and Aunt Sharon—your kids—to say good bye. I know you are near the end...but please...I beg you, please hold on..."

Beep. Beep. Beep. Once again, my prayers were answered. I can't make this stuff up. I was truly blown away that she came back.

The phone rang at the nurses' station. It was my mom to let me know that she was on her way.

With urgency I said, "Mom, grandma's dying. I'm alone. Please hurry. She's flat lined twice already. I don't know how much longer she has...please hurry."

"I have to pick up your brothers and we'll be there soon. Gene is on his way. Sharon can't make it. Tell her how much I love her, and ask her to hang in there. You hang in there, too. I'll be there as fast as I can," she said, rushing to get off the phone to be at her mom's side before it was too late.

I returned to my grandma.

"Grandma, Mom and Gene are on their way. She loves you. Please hold on. I'm gonna go have a smoke—I'll be right back."

Though it was probably the last thing I should do, I couldn't deal with the feelings. Drinking wasn't an option. I went back to my little private balcony and choked down two more cigarettes while I tried to process all that had happened in the past forty-five minutes.

I stopped briefly to use the restroom and wash my face and hands before returning to my grandmother's side. I glanced into the mirror. I looked like an emotional wreck. I was. I took a few deep breaths, and returned to her room. She lay still, lifeless. Her gaunt face was wrinkled by years of smoking. Yet, she looked at peace. The heart monitor beeped regularly. *Thank God.*

Running out of things to say, I decided to share some of my thoughts with her—it wasn't a true confessional, but, I had at least another half hour until my mom and uncle would arrive.

I told her how glad I was for *not* selling me her Chevelle when I was seventeen—as fast as that car was, I probably would've died in a car crash. I apologized for driving her Cutlass drunk. I talked about the stories my mom had told me of how tough it was for Grandpa dealing with his father's suicide.

I held her hand, hoping for some response…for some indication that she was listening…instead the heart monitor blared as her heart rate climbed to 120….The shrill of the monitor pierced my eardrums.

"No!" I cried. "Grandma, I'm sorry. I am so sorry. Was it too much?" I cried out, feeling guilty about bringing up the story about my grandpa. "You can't go yet! I know you are there. You can hear me. Please, just a bit longer. Mom is on her way…Nurse!" Rene quickly appeared. She frowned, seeing the inevitable.

Just then, above the shriek of the EKG monitor, I heard the phone ringing at the nurses' station.

"Hello, ICU, " another nurse answered the phone. "Yes, you best hurry!" she urged.

The nurse entered the room. "That was your mom. She's in the lobby with your brothers and on her way up."

"Henri," Rene called out to my grandmother. "Your daughter is here. She'll be by your side in a few minutes.... Please come back, if you can," Rene said, gently squeezing Grandma's hand.

"Grandma, you can do it. I know you can.... Just a few more minutes, then you can say goodbye to all of us," I implored her again grasping her hand. I felt her fingers grip my hand firmly. As she squeezed, she came back to life, for the third time.

The elevator doors opened down the hall. My mom rushed down to her mother's bedside. Tears streamed down her face.

"Momma! Momma! We're here," she announced, doing her best to be strong.

I felt like a ton of bricks was lifted off my shoulders as soon as my mom approached. I'd just been part of something miraculous. Coaxing. Praying. Begging and pleading for my own grandmother to come back from the dead. Not once, not twice, but three times.

"Oh Momma," my mom embraced her own mother as she would a child. "I love you, Momma. I love you!" She rocked Grandma as she would a sleeping baby. Brushing her silver locks as she kissed her forehead.

"Gene will be here soon. I love you, Momma. Seth and Kelly are here, too. Come here, boys," she said, inviting us closer. She buried her head on my shoulder and sobbed.

Life goes by so very fast. We come into this world dependent on another for our survival. We live, and then, in the blink of an eye it ends. Some of us are fortunate enough to say goodbye to a loved one before they move on. Others aren't so lucky. On this day, we were blessed that God saw fit to keep Grandma alive so we all could say our goodbyes.

I believe that the spirit of those we love will always be near to our hearts. It's okay to talk to them, to think about them, to say a prayer that you are thinking of them, love them, miss them, and hope that they are well.

In the end, all that really matters is love. Love of a mother for their child. A child for a parent. A brother for a brother or sister, husbands and wives, strangers and friends. In this moment as we encircled my grandmother, I could feel that love—a presence, unlike any other— a feeling of peace.

My mother chatted to my grandmother, comforting her and letting go as she told her how much she loved her.

Ten to fifteen minutes later, my uncle arrived.

"How is she?" he asked, looking at my mom, then me.

"Not good, Gene," my mom said, throwing her arms around her twin brother, weeping. He stood 6'3" and was built like a quarterback. He was always her protector, even as a kid.

"She's waiting for you to say goodbye," she said, still holding onto my uncle. "Shawn said she flat lined three times already…"

"Wow," Gene said, shaking his head in disbelief, then letting go of my mom before going to my grandmother's side. "Hi, Ma," he said. "You don't look so hot." Usually this would entice a smirk from my grandma. Today, there was none. Her eyes were closed, her breath was rattling—slow—deliberate.

Bending over her to kiss her on the forehead, my uncle continued his goodbye, "Well, I made it. Sharon can't get here. All the kids and Nancy want you to know how much you are loved. Joannie's here with the boys, and we all want to say we love you. If you are ready to go meet your husband in Heaven, go when you want."

We encircled her bed, held hands and without even thinking of it, said goodbye.

She gasped her final breath and let go.

The EKG monitor went flat for the last time.

Rene came by to give her condolences and to say that we could have our time to say final goodbyes before they would take her downstairs to the morgue. She disconnected all the leads and monitors. The room was silent.

That was one of the toughest things I went through in early recovery. I didn't have to drink over any of it. The sequence of events that transpired taught me a couple lessons that I have drawn upon many times hence: to not fear death and to trust that God is with us—always.

Chapter 16
Anger Therapy

With alcohol gone, I struggled to process my emotions in a healthy way. Shortly after my angry outburst at the Mexican restaurant and whining to my sponsor over women and jealousy issues, he suggested I start seeing a therapist.

I started therapy and had made some progress dealing with some of my abandonment and anger issues. But therapy is like peeling an onion, there is always another layer.

Now, as I sat in the reception area of my therapists office in Sausalito, waiting for his 1 p.m. appointment to finish. The door opened, and my therapist, TJ, said goodbye to his client, then invited me in.

TJ was a thin man, a distance runner and bicyclist, with a moustache and soft spoken voice.

"Have a seat," he said as he gestured to the chair in the corner of his office. I sat and glanced out the window that overlooked the San Francisco Bay.

"How you doing?" He asked.

"Good." I replied, distracted briefly by the sailboat on the bay.

"We've come to the point where I think you are close to a break through," he stated. "You've talked a lot about some of the past anger over your dad—how his leaving created abandonment issues and jealousy issues, fear of intimacy, and how drugs and alcohol helped you for a time, but those stopped working. And now that you're sober for what?"

"Almost three years," I beamed.

"Three years—that's fantastic! Some of these repressed feelings are surfacing and you need a safe way to release them. You've had a few situations like the Mexican restaurant where you just snapped."

"Yeah—I'm really sorry that I did that."

"Yes, but in some way it probably felt good right?" he grinned.

I paused, thinking, *Why would he suggest that it felt good?* "Yeah, it felt really good at the time!" I smiled, flashing back to that evening.

His look turned serious. "Last week, I told you that we were going to dig a little deeper to get closer to the core of your anger and jealousy issues, especially those around your father and dating," he reminded me.

I nodded then thought, *Do I really want to get into this now?* I'd spent the past two years working on stuff with him. I felt like I had made major improvements. I was apprehensive and beginning to have second thoughts where this may be going.

"Have you heard of biokinetic therapy?" TJ asked.

"No. What's that?" I asked, sitting up straight.

He went on to explain, "In its simplest form, it is a way to kinetically get down to our deepest core emotions to free them so we can heal more completely."

"What does that mean?—How?" I asked.

"I'll show you but, it's very important to do this in a safe place when the patient is ready. It's also very important that you be able to trust in the process and commit one hundred percent to it," he stated.

I trusted him. Taking his cue that this was something important, I nodded and leaned forward. Still not quite sure what it entailed, or how it would help, I listened intently.

"Here's how it works," he picked up to a two foot square foam cube covered with red and blue fabric and set it down in front of him. Then he grabbed a tennis racket to demonstrate. "What I want you to do is stand with your legs shoulder width, knees bent, then take a few deep breaths to get balanced. Grip the racket handle firmly and raise it over your head. Think of whatever the first thing is that comes to mind about your dad that makes you angry. Like this." He gripped the racket, to demonstrate, with feet spread shoulder width, knees bent. He took three deep breaths, then raised the racket over his head. "I'm angry at my first ex-wife because she left me for another man, " he growled as he smacked the cube—*Thwack!* He did it again…"I'm angry at my first ex-wife because she spent all my money!" *Whack!* And again. Each blow to the cube more intense. I could see his emotions coming to the surface—his face was red with anger and rage, followed by a moment of sadness.

"You get the idea?" he asked, wiping the sweat from his brow with the back of his sleeve.

"Yeah," I grinned, thinking, *This is going to be fun.*

"Start slowly," he cautioned. "Understand that as you continue you may tap into some deep-seated anger. It's okay. That's what we want. It's safe. Let it surface. Pound it all out through the racket into the cube as hard as you want!" TJ grinned. I think he was excited to see where this may go.

I did as he instructed. I stood, gripped the tennis racket, took a few deep breaths, then raised it over my head…

"I'm angry about my dad leaving us!" *Whack!* I slammed the tennis racket into the cube. Again, arms raised. "I'm angry at my dad …" *Thwap!* "for not saying goodbye!" Anger welled up. My jaw tightened. My whole body was wound tight. I was getting sweaty.

I could feel the pain rising up through my arms and out the head of the tennis racket as I continued to slam the racket into the cube.

"That's good, Shawn," TJ said. "Continue, only now I want you to picture your dad there."

Racket up. Feet planted, "Why did you run away?!"…*Whack!* "You fucking coward!"

"Again…HARDER!" he exhorted me.

"I hate you!" *Thwack!* "I wish you'd die!" *Whack, Whack, Whack!*

Then I dropped into a zone…. "I see you laughing…you think…" *Whack* "…it's…" *Whack* "…funny?!" *Whack, whack.* Then I pounded it with clenched fists. "Use the racket," TJ reminded me.

"You never gave my mom a dime!" *Smack!* "You're just another deadbeat dad!"

I could feel sweat dripping down my face.

"Cool, Shawn, keep going. Tell him how you feel. Let it all out."

At his coaching, I unleashed all my anger, every last ounce of fiery rage I had been holding on to for so long. I beat the living crap out of that cube with the racket. It was safe. I had permission to let it all out, all that pressure that I had stuffed for so long that was eating me alive from the inside out began to dissipate and release with every thump.

"I hate that you never got to be there for my graduation! That you wouldn't play catch with me! It's all your fault that we had to live so poor! Didn't you love us?" *Whack!* "How could you turn your back on your family? Why? What happened? Why did you leave?" *Whack! Whack! Whack!* The masks of *I have it all together* and *I can handle this* were ripped away as I pounded the crap out of that foam cube.

I tapped into and released rage that had been buried deep inside. Raw kinetic energy exploded like a volcano from the depths of my body, mind, and soul, out through the racket and transferred safely into that two foot foam cube. The demons that haunted me had been exorcised. I was left with deep regret and sadness. It hurt that he left and didn't seem to care for my mom, my younger brothers, or me. I felt sorry for him. He missed so much!

I broke down and sobbed, dropping to my knees and letting go of the tennis racket.

"Let it go Shawn. Let it all flow out…you're doing great!"

"Oh, Dad! I miss you! I just wanted to know that you love us. Why did you have to go? We had so much more to do, and you threw it all away. What did we do? Why couldn't you stay?"

Loud deep sobs…guttural soul cleansing. Keening, with my knees pulled up to my chest in a fetal position, rocking.

"All I wanted to know was that you loved us! I still love, you dad! I still love you and want to spend more time with you. But it hurts…it hurts so bad." More tears streamed down my face. In my sorrow I also felt cleansed. I could sense the broken parts inside me slowly mending. I had surrendered to the whole process and now, for the first time, I felt like I could finally move forward.

"Shawn, you did it! That's wonderful. How do you feel?" TJ asked, handing me a box of tissues. I wiped my eyes and blew my nose. I caught my breath.

"I feel much better!" I said, then admitted, "There's probably more."

"There probably is," he said with a consoling smile, "but that's great work for today. I think you have made a huge breakthrough. Now we can start the road to healing."

I hugged him, "Thank you! I feel like I've dropped a ton of bricks off my back."

"You have, Shawn. You have. See you next week."

Chapter 17
Looking for Love

On my one year sobriety birthday, I decided to treat myself to a trip to Hawaii. I invited my college buddy, Duane, and in January of 1988, we climbed on a plane for Oahu. I'll never forget the smell of the tuberose leis and the sweet salty air as we exited the plane in Oahu. I felt like I was in Heaven.

We found our hotel right on the beach in Waikiki and settled in. The next day, he introduced me to me to his uncle, a very successful business man on Oahu, and his aunt, a beautiful Polynesian woman, as well as his two cousins. They were consummate hosts and spoiled us rotten for a couple days. We meet at their gorgeous home overlooking Pearl Harbor, and, after a brief tour, left for dinner in their Rolls Royce. They had arranged front row seats at a traditional Hawaiian luau, complete with roast pig and poi. They all enjoyed several Mai Tais and Blue Hawaiians, and convinced me and Duane to get on stage for public hula lessons. The next evening, they treated us to steak and lobster at Outback Steakhouse. After dinner, we thanked them for their generosity, and parted ways.

Over the next few days, Duane and I snorkeled at Hanauma Bay State Park, boogie boarded at Waikiki Beach, and visited Waimea State park where we toured the lush gardens and watched cliff diving at Waimea Falls.

There at Waimea Falls, as we watched divers do flips and pikes off thirty foot cliffs, I felt someone sit behind me. A woman I'd never met before was now straddling me, completely uninhibited, her legs wrapped on the outside of mine. I turned my head to look at her. She was very voluptuous wearing a white one-piece swimsuit that left little to the imagination. Our eyes locked. There were no words, just a knowing grin that said enough. She pressed her chest against my back and wrapped her arms around my waist. As soon as the divers had finished their show, she led me out to the pools. We swam out to the base of the waterfall. "Hi, I'm Shawn," I said to her as the water cascaded over us both. *I can't believe this is happening*, I thought.

"I'm Rachel," she said, reaching into my shorts. Few words were spoken. We were lost in our own world, lost in lust. Everyone around us vanished. The tourists around the falls and all else seemed to fade away as we embraced passionately.

We swam back to the shore and she invited me to drive her white convertible Mustang rental car. I let Duane know that I would be going and would see him later. With the top down and my new friend in the passenger seat, we headed to Hanauma Bay in rush hour traffic, and spent the next five hours lost in lustful passion.

I finally returned at 11 p.m. Duane was pissed. He had no idea where I was and told me he had been ready to call the Honolulu Police because he thought I was dead or something. I was too preoccupied to bother calling. I apologized for causing him to worry, then told him all about my sexcapade.

The next few years of sobriety were a complete blur. Sure, I had stopped drinking, but I felt like a hormonal teenager, and was living every day in the moment; it would be a while before I moved past that phase. Not long after Hawaii, I asked my friend, Ben, if he could take me to San Diego to pick up my stuff from storage. His ex-girlfriend from high school, Jill, lived in Huntington Beach and made arrangements for us to stay with her and her roommate, Cynthia, for a day before going all the way to San Diego. We grabbed some candy and two thirty-two ounce mugs of coffee, and took off at midnight. By the time we hit Patterson on Highway 5, the fog was so thick we could barely see the road. Then a Camaro flew by us at about 100 m.p.h. Without hesitation, Ben punched it. The engine of his 1978 V-8 Cutlass Supreme roared as we chased the taillights of the speeding Camaro. We were hauling ass. I glanced at the speedometer—100...115...120...and started to get nervous. We quickly closed in on the taillights of the Camaro. As Ben pulled alongside them, they took off. We chased for a bit longer then let them go. It was a rush, but scared the crap out of me.

After a couple of hours of sleep on the side of the road, we rolled into Huntington Beach around 8 a.m. Both Jill and Cynthia were sweet and attractive. We grabbed a bite to eat at a local diner, then they both headed to work. Ben and I spent the day at the beach before reconnecting with them at their house that evening.

Ben was a charmer, I was shy. Regardless, I hit it off with Cynthia and ended up dating her for several months after that. I liked her a lot. She had a good heart and was smart.

And she had a good job. She liked me, too and would fly up to spend weekends with me twice a month.

One night after work, she handed me a small box wrapped in silver paper. Inside was a framed copy of the serenity poem I had written and given her. She had taken it to Kinko's and had it typeset. It looked so beautiful.

Serenity

Serenity is soft like a warm summer breeze
Serenity is the warmth of a fire on a cold winters day
Serenity smells like the blossoms of spring
Serenity is radiant like the setting sun
Serenity is peace when we are alone
Serenity has a place in my heart and my home
Serenity is a friendly smile when we feel blue
Serenity is acceptance of things as they are
Serenity is a phone call from a friend afar
Serenity is love of myself and my friends
Serenity is a feeling that doesn't have to end
Shawn Langwell -1987

Her loving gesture brought me to tears. I saw her heart. She showed me love. I will forever be grateful to her for that. I felt like I was falling for her, but was torn. The distance between us made it challenging to maintain a long distance relationship and I was young, naïve, and still newly sober. I wasn't sure if I was ready to settle down. In many ways, I was a teenager in the body of a twenty-three-year-old, and not ready to commit to more. Shortly thereafter, we parted ways. She was crushed and I felt lousy.

Afraid to Commit

Even though I was staying sober, and making great progress with respect to my anger issues, I was still in denial about my fear of intimacy. I would go out dancing virtually every night in the hopes of meeting someone, or at least to burn off some energy by grinding it out on the dance floor to popular dance hits like, Salt-N-Pepa, *Push It*, or Bobby Brown, *Every Little Step*, and so many more. Sometimes I'd go with a bunch of sober friends or work colleagues, but usually I went alone after work and danced until closing. My sponsor later told me he didn't think I would stay sober, because I was basically partying every night—only without the booze. I drank non-alcoholic beers like they were water. I loved dancing. It was a great release, but it got old.

Since Hawaii and Huntington beach, I was doing what many addicts do—"switching seats on the Titanic"—a common euphemism in addiction. I used sex as an escape.

After a series of several failed relationships, trysts, and one night stands, over the first two and a half years of sobriety, I finally gave up. I stopped going out for a period of time. My motives were all selfish. A hopeless romantic, I prayed about finding the right someone. I wanted to find a wife and start a family, I just didn't know who or where.

On a whim, I went back to the night club after work on a Friday night. It was packed, as usual, but I knew a few people there. Melanie, the woman I'd briefly dated from the Mexican restaurant, was there with a couple girlfriends—Vicky, who I knew from high school and recovery, and Adele, an attractive blonde, who I'd never met. They were roommates. We all danced for a while. When Adele and her roommate left for the restroom, Melanie whispered in my ear, "You know she's got the hots for you."

I smiled. "Really? Adele?"

"Yep," she said with a huge grin.

We talked and danced, and I found out she went to Drake High at the same time as me, but our paths never crossed in high school—she was hanging in the parking lot with the cool kids smoking; I was in the bleachers getting stoned.

She drove me back to my apartment and parked, and then we made out in the car. As we were kissing, a drunken man knocked on our window asking for a ride. We moved around the corner parked again. He must have followed us, because we heard another tap on the window, "Hey can I get a ride?" he slurred, sticking out his thumb. We drove around the block again.

Here's where I nearly blew it. I invited her up to shower, clearly with ulterior motives. She said that wasn't a good idea. I nodded—I had not yet learned the proper way to court a lady.

"You're right," I agreed, opening the door to leave.

"Well, aren't you going to ask for my number?" she asked. I was afraid of getting close. We had just met. I was afraid of being vulnerable. Guys really are thick sometimes, at least in that moment I was.

"Uh, yeah!" I exclaimed, feeling embarrassed that I didn't ask first.

Two days later, I worked up the courage to call her. Her roommate answered. Since I knew her roommate, Vicky, I picked her brain to build up my courage before I talked to Adele. The next thing I knew, Adele and I were dating. I really liked her and didn't want to screw it up, so I later asked my sponsor for advice.

"Take her for a walk in Sausalito," he said. "Get to know her. And don't sleep with her yet."

I did exactly as he said and took it slow. We went for a stroll along the water in Sausalito and had lunch at Houlihans.

Shortly after that she moved into a new apartment in Fairfax. I got to meet her mom and dad when I helped her move.

Two weeks later, I invited her to the San Francisco Comedy Competition in Golden Gate Park where we got to see, Robin Williams, Ellen DeGeneres, George Lopez, Michael Pritchard, and many more famous comedians. It was a blast.

That was July of 1989. After that, I spent nearly every free moment at her apartment.

Later that fall, my roommate and friend from recovery wanted to go on a ski trip to Tahoe. The Giants and A's were playing in World Series at nearby Candlestick Park while we waited at the San Francisco Airport for a six o'clock flight to Tahoe. On October 17, 1989 at 5:04 p.m., a violent earthquake hit the Bay Area. This was by far the most powerful earthquake I had experienced—a 6.9 on the Richter scale. It felt like we were in the spin cycle of an unbalanced load of laundry. Looking for a spot to "duck and cover," I turned to run toward a row of plastic chairs along the wall of windows on the terminal side of the gate, but the undulating floor knocked me off balance. I staggered toward the windows and curled up under the false safety of the plastic chairs while I watched ceiling tiles bounce off my friends who had hugged the center stations of the waiting area. I prayed for our safety, and that the windows wouldn't shatter and decapitate me. Then it stopped. None of us were hurt, but we were all in shock. It was like a zombie movie as hundreds of travelers wandered about the airport in a daze. A crowd formed around the banks of payphones. We stood in line waiting our turn.

After several attempts, each of us were able to get through to our families to see how they were and let them know we were okay. I was also able to reach my uncle who lives near the San Francisco Airport, and he agreed to put us up for the night. The next day the airport was clear and we made it to Tahoe.

When I came back, Adele and I realized that we were getting serious and decided to move in together. Right after high school, I had taken a goal setting class at College of Marin. From this class, I knew the best way to find the perfect apartment was to write out a list of what we wanted. I pulled out one of the goal sheets from my goal binder and began dreaming.

Growing up in Marin, I always wanted to have a home with a view of Mount Tamalpais, a majestic mountain rising above the hills and slopes of Mill Valley and Marin with a silhouette that has earned it the nickname, "The Sleeping Lady."

Here's the goal I wrote down for our ideal apartment:

I wanted a top floor apartment with vaulted ceilings and a fireplace, pool and rec room. It would be on a hill next to open space with a view of Mount Tam. It needed to be clean and quiet with covered parking.

I read through the list and the affirmation statements, and began to picture what it would be like to watch the sun set behind Mount Tam from the comfort of our dining room or living room. My goal and dream was now crystal clear.

A year earlier, I had written a similar list and affirmation for who I would want for a mate. I imagined the details and set my subconscious mind to work. Now the goals and affirmations had truly become real. I was with the woman I had envisioned—kind, attractive and with a good heart—and we had found the ideal apartment —the top floor of a one-bedroom + den on a hill, next to open space, with a view of Tam, and it had a pool, rec room and even a fireplace! It was perfect.

After we moved in, I continued to commute to school by bus three to four days a week to finish earning my B.S. in Business Administration at San Francisco State University while working five nights a week at Ristorante Italia as a waiter. She continued her career as an R.D.A. (registered dental assistant) and C.D.A. (certified dental assistant) for a local orthodontist office. We were "living the dream." Then I got greedy—I had come so far in early sobriety, but had not yet established credit. She agreed to co-sign for a joint credit card that I quickly maxed out from cash advances. I was gambling—betting on horses, football and playing poker in an effort to save up money for an engagement ring. Bad idea. She gave me an ultimatum, "Give it up or you're out." I gave it up. This became one more short-lived addiction I fortunately got over before it got worse.

We had talked of marriage and wanting to raise a family. My long-term goal was to get married, own a home with a white picket fence, and have two to three kids. One night around Adele's birthday, we invited her parents over for dinner. Before dinner I was on my knees stoking the fire, I took the opportunity to ask her father's permission to marry his daughter. He didn't respond. When Adele asked him the next day, he said, "No one is good enough for my daughter."

Chapter 18
Young Hormones

In early June of 1991, my friend Benny was getting married. One of his closest friends insisted on a traditional bachelor party—a *real* bachelor party, as he put it—the kind with strippers, food, and a keg—even though several of us didn't drink.

The apartment complex where I lived had a very nice rec room. It had plenty of room for twenty guys, and was the perfect space for a bachelor party. It had wet bar area, bathrooms, a separate dressing area for the entertainment, and a big screen TV to watch the NBA Finals between the Lakers and Bulls.

Seth and a couple of his friends helped me get set up. We lined up twenty or so folding chairs around the room, leaving the center of the room open for the dancers. It didn't take long, so we watched the NBA Finals while getting a head start on the food as we waited for the entertainment and other guests to arrive. That series was an intense battle that included several future Hall of Famers on both teams: Michael Jordan and Scotty Pippen of the Bulls, and Magic Johnson, James Worthy, and Vlade Divac of the Lakers. We saw as much of the game as we could before Benny and his best friend, Joe, showed up, followed by Ben's father.

Ben was a sharp guy, a charmer. He had a way about him that enabled him to bullshit his way out of or into situations.

Several years prior, when we were going out to a sober dance in Fairfax, he had gotten pulled over by a cop. He had an air of confidence about him that I'd never seen. Now most people would stay put behind the wheel. But not him.

"Wait here, I got this," he said to me.

I was shocked. He slowly opened the door of his car, got out, and walked toward the cop. The cops spot light trained right in his eye.

"Get back in the ca...." the cop started, "Oh, hey Benny—I didn't know it was you."

"Yeah—what'd you stop me for Nick?" Ben asked.

"You ran the stop sign."

"Oh, shit," he chuckled. "How's Michelle and the kids?"

"Fine. What're you up to?"

"Oh, just going up to the sober dance on the hill. I quit three years ago."

"That's great, no more wild parties, eh?"

"I quit, but I'm not dead. I've been having more fun these past years than ever before, and I don't wake up hung over. Sorry about the stop sign."

"Don't worry about it. Just don't let it happen again," Nick said.

Now, a few years later we celebrated his final send off before getting remarried. His friend has insisted on giving him a "real bachelor party." He was a good sport about it.

Over twenty guys showed up and the show was about to begin. Donna Summer's "Bad Boys" played. "Gentlemen let's get this party started," the DJ bellowed into a microphone— "Heeere's Candy!"

Candy sauntered in with a bad girl attitude, twirling a nightstick and a switch. She was a gorgeous brunette, dressed in a cop uniform, black Daisy Dukes, fishnets, and stiletto heels. She paraded around the room, taunting and teasing with her switch before making her way to the guest of honor in the center of the room. Ben's dad stood and slipped a twenty dollar bill into the waistband of her tight shorts. She made a move toward the old man, but he shook his head and pointed back to his son. As she sauntered over to the bachelor, the DJ switched the song to "Private Dancer" while she gave him a not-so-private dance. Then, eyeing my brother whose tongue was practically on the floor, she made her way over to him. Seth was a big boy—6' tall, 220 lbs. with a 17" neck, and a flirty smirk that made him well liked by many young women. He slipped $10 in her top and she gave him a short dance before continuing to "work" the room.

"Private Dancer" ended and was followed by that all too familiar hit, "Brick House."

"Gentlemen, this party is just getting started. Give it up for Mandy!" the energetic DJ continued. As if on cue, every head in the room swiveled as the tall blonde made her sultry entrance. She strutted in wearing a red and black ruffled plaid skirt, white knee high stockings, and patent leather shoes. She held a finger to her lips, a secret smile in her eyes while she paraded around the room.

Shortly thereafter, Candy re-entered with a can of whipped cream in her hand, wearing a g-string, and stiletto heels. *Oh no,* I thought. I'd never been at a bachelor party before, and had told my fiancé that it would be tame. I could see now that it was bound to get out of control. The hard body dancers continued to work the room, squirting whipped cream everywhere. Fortunately, the beer ran out just before the last dance. The party was over. The DJ took control and thanked everyone, while the dancers gathered their strewn garments—bras, g-strings, whips, toys, and feather boas. People started to leave, but some lingered. Two of the bachelor's friends were pretty wasted. One bumped a coffee table and knocked over a lamp. The other staggered by the front door and knocked a picture off the wall, nearly shattering it.

"Guys, it's time to go," I said politely. "The party's over."

"We want more dancing!" one of them slurred. They both started toward the bathroom where the girls were changing.

"Guys, time to go—party's over," I repeated, standing between them and the bathroom.

One of them puffed his chest out as if to pick a fight. My younger brother was watching the whole thing.

"We all had a great time. Keg's out. Party's over. Time to go before anything gets broken," I said again.

"Broken?!" the larger of the two mocked me, "you mean like this?" He belligerently swatted the table lamp. It fell over, popping the bulb as it hit the ground. Tiny shards spilled to the floor.

"It's time to go! NOW!" I raised my voice. Not wanting a bigger scene, I put my hands on their shoulders and guided them to the door. That set them off. They resisted, and both spun around to make their way to the bathroom where the dancers were changing.

"We're not ready to go. What are you gonna do about it?!" The shorter one with a buzz cut and a broken heart tattoo on his bicep said as he pushed me against the wall.

Oh shit, I thought. *Just what I was afraid of...*

In an instant, Seth, who had been keeping a watchful eye on both of them, bounded over the small step near the entry, grabbed each one of them by the neck—one in each hand—and slammed them against the wall, lifting them off their feet.

"Nobody touches my brother, motherfuckers!" he growled. "It's time to go. He asked you nicely. Now if you don't want me to rip your fucking heads off, I suggest you go—now!" he shouted and threw them down the landing toward the door.

Just then, a San Rafael Police officer pulled up—*Perfect timing or not,* I thought, as he parked his patrol car and walked toward the door. Not wanting to risk arrest, the two guys walked right past the officer. One of their sober friends followed.

"They aren't driving are they?" the cop asked.

"No, I got 'em, " their sober friend said, grabbing each of them by the shoulders and leading them away from trouble.

The officer nodded, then turned toward the door of the rec room, "Everything alright here?"

"All good, Officer. We're all done here," Ben said.

"Well, we had complaint of noise," the officer said, scanning the room.

"It was my bachelor party, I'm getting married tomorrow."

"Well, good for you. But it's time to break it up."

"We're done—just cleaning up," Ben said.

The officer waited for all of us to leave.

My brother, his friends, and I cleaned up, while the dancers gathered their things and left.

"Goodnight ladies," Seth said with raised eyebrows.

They smiled, winked, said goodnight, and left.

School's out for Summer

Later that summer, the streets and sidewalks in downtown San Rafael were brimming with "young hormones," as my mom referred to teenagers. Gorgeous girls in tight shorts and tube tops flipped their platinum blonde and brunette manes, teasing the equally fit and toned boys, flirting shamelessly as teens often do.

I was serving customers on the patio of Ristorante Italia on Fourth Street in San Rafael where I had worked for the past five years. The patio had been enclosed with huge sliding glass doors that served as windows so we could use the space in the winter to seat diners. It was one of the "in" restaurants in town. But this night, it was warm and the windows were fully opened.

"Beep! Beep!" A horn squeaked from a motorcycle. I looked up. "Hey, brosheem!"

My brother Seth was riding a wheelie on his Red and White XL 250 down Fourth street.

He was bare-chested, showing off his untanned torso and wearing a shit-eating grin.

"Check out that ass!" he said, nodding in the direction of a very cute blonde wearing tight white shorts. I smiled. "Hey baby! Wanna ride?" he called to her. "I'm the Wheelie King....Wheee!" He hit the horn again and let go of the handlebars.

"Look bro, no hands! Ha! Ha!" This was followed by a shrill siren. The San Rafael police didn't think it was so funny.

"Pull over and park the bike," the officer announced over the loudspeaker. My brother looked my way, shrugging his shoulders, as he smirked. He hit the brakes, dropping the front wheel to the ground. Then he flashed another grin, revved the throttle, popped the clutch, and rode through the red light on his back wheel, hit the brakes to drop the front wheel, then took off like a bat-outta-hell! He had no fear. I found out later that he flew through the maze of downtown streets, hit the back-roads, then safely hid the bike in my mom's garage in Fairfax.

Not long after that, he would pay me another visit. "Brosheem! Check out my wrist!" he boasted, holding up his casted left arm. I dropped the check for the last guests of my lunch shift and went outside to say hey.

"How did you do that?" I asked.

"Poppin' a wheelie!" he grinned.

I smiled and chuckled, "Figures."

"Yeah I was pulling a no-hander and checking out a hottie when I ran into a car!" he laughed. "It'll be fine.... I can still use my fingers." He wiggled four fingers on his left hand.

I smiled—just being around him even for five minutes made me smile.

"Bummer, too," he continued. "That girl was so fine, she liked me. I wanted to give her the root!"

I raised my eyebrows wondering what the hell he meant.

"You know the root!" he gestured to his groin. "The root, the whole root, and nothing but the root!" He bellowed out a loud laugh as he demonstrated with a spinning gesture by his crotch…"Spin her like a top!" I coughed, laughing so hard I nearly peed my pants. Sick? Yes. Sexist? Yeah. But he was so charming that you couldn't help but laugh. Only my brother could come up with a description like that, and, as crude as it was, that shit was funny!

"Gotta go mow some lawns!" he said giving me a hug. "Later!"

"Bye! Love ya. Be careful," I said to my little brother.

"Never!" he laughed. He revved his engine, popped a wheelie, and was off.

Chapter 19
Just Say Yes!

During a phone conversation one evening, my mom told me about her visions to meet a kind and wonderful man. She said that he was out there, she just didn't know where. Well, her vision came to fruition and she met David O'Connor, one of the kindest, smartest, wittiest, and caring men I've known. They would be moving in together and wanted to know if Adele and I wanted to take over the lease of the house she was renting in Fairfax. This was too perfect, it even had a white picket fence. Of course we said yes, just as she would when her new beau proposed to her two years later. That would be the headline on their wedding invitations:

She said, "YES!"

My stepfather, became someone I looked up to, not just as a father figure but as a mentor. I have the utmost respect for him. He worked in advertising for over forty years, fought in WWII and the Korean War as a fighter pilot, and has always seemed upbeat and positive, willing to offer advice when asked and, occasionally, when unsolicited. But then again, many guys are like that—trying to offer free advice or solve problems. It's how we're wired.

I was at the finish line for school, but really was at the starting gate for the rest of my life. After ten years of school interrupted by a lifesaving hiatus to get sober, I would be graduating in May, which, due to unforeseen circumstances with classes, was scheduled on the same day as my wedding. My decision was easy—I would walk the aisle to get married instead of attend the graduation ceremony.

Though I had normal pre-wedding jitters, I was confident in the decision to marry. I was also preoccupied about how to develop a career beyond food service. I had mastered the art of waiting tables and serving customers and was very good at it. It represented comfort and familiarity.

In my gut, though, I knew I had to spread my wings and venture into the unknown; to put my education to work and pursue a career in business, marketing, or advertising, but I had no idea where to start. I was stuck. I had so many questions: *Did I want to work for an agency, or for a company on the client side, or media? What kind of marketing and advertising jobs should I pursue? Did I want to sell advertising, products, services or go into marketing?* There was no internet to search, no blogs, no career site, and no Craigslist. Instead, I sought out advice from my stepdad, Dave—the one person who had experience in this arena, and whom I respected and trusted.

We sat on the deck of his hillside home in Forest Knolls and had a conversation that I would reflect on many times hence.

He asked me point blank, "What are you afraid of?"

"I don't know."

He asked again, "What are you afraid of?"

After a long pause, "I don't know, maybe failure."

"What else?" he prodded.

I racked my brain searching for the answer I thought he wanted, but nothing came to mind. I paused and asked myself the question.

"Success," I admitted, though it felt weird like an oxymoron. *Why would anyone be afraid of success?*

"Ha!" he exclaimed with his unique laugh. "And why would you be afraid of success?" I thought about his question for a moment and paused, hoping he'd give me a few ideas to choose from.

"Because it's something new, I guess?" I said, not sure this was the answer he was looking for.

We continued for fifteen to twenty minutes discussing how we are all successful at something—that most success or failure is a product of our perception of our abilities, and the best way to become successful is through practice—trying something to see if it works. If it doesn't, then try doing it differently or try something else. Ultimately, we agreed that fear of success or failure is really tied to the fear of the unknown and the fear of change.

"What's the worst that could happen?" he tossed the question out there for me to chew on.

"I don't know," I said.

"Die?" he prompted me.

"Nah, I'll succeed or find a way that didn't work." I shook my head, then sat up straight.

"Yeah—anything wrong with that?" he probed further.

I shrugged my shoulders. "No, I guess not."

"So, there's nothing to be afraid of is there?" he added with a wry but loving grin.

I shook my head.

"So, what do you want to do?" he asked, leaning in closer.

"I don't know…" Deadpan, I stared across the deck to Mount Barnabe as I contemplated his question.

Though our conversation was relatively short, I never forgot it. He didn't solve my problem for me, instead he coached me to think about how *I* could solve it. I was afraid of making the wrong decision and stuck in indecision; analysis paralysis as I call it.

The lesson I learned that day is that most fears are false. They're based on what we think may or may not happen. Afraid of making the wrong decision, I concluded that the best antidote for indecision is to try *something*.

I took his advice to heart and went to work searching the classifieds for a job in advertising. I applied to agencies, big and small—from newspapers like The Press Democrat or Marin IJ, to any company in the Bay Area that was hiring for marketing or advertising.

In January, I received a call from the classified manager, Robin, of Mix Magazine and Electronic Musician. The next day we met for an interview.

She was a thin, direct woman with sparkling green and brown eyes, pale skin, and a mane of curly red hair. She asked some good questions and said that there were a couple other candidates that they were considering, and that she'd be in touch.

A few days later, I received another call and was offered the job. I was excited until she told me the salary —$18k per year with full benefits—far less than I was making as a waiter. I asked if I could sleep on it. I ended up calling her back the next day to accept, as long as I'd be able to take a week off for my honeymoon in May. She agreed. I would start in two weeks. To maintain the same income I had as a waiter, I held on to two shifts a week at the restaurant for the first few months.

I was so lost after the first day at the magazine, and after two weeks, I almost quit. I knew nothing about the music business, or the recording gear I was writing ad copy for. I could barely type, yet my manager believed in me and taught me how to sell. I stuck it out, and that summer the publisher offered me an opportunity to help sell and renew clients for an annual awards program. That was a huge lift in commission, and it enabled me to let go of the restaurant job. From there, I earned promotions, raises, and never looked back for the next ten years.

The Big Day

Our wedding was quickly approaching and things were coming together on schedule. Adele and I initially were going to do a potluck and keep it all low key, but Adele's mom and dad would not have any part of a potluck. They insisted on paying for all the food and hosted beverages. After looking at several sites, Adele and I found a church on the top of Rock Hill Drive in Tiburon overlooking the Bay, with a view of the Golden Gate Bridge in the background. It was perfect.

The morning of the wedding, I was climbing the walls. Bobby, my best man, and Melton were supposed to be at the house by 10 a.m. for breakfast, and they were purposely late—they wanted to ruffle my feathers a little, said it built character. I didn't find it amusing, but it all worked out.

We had a huge breakfast and joked around while getting dressed. Our pastor had suggested I eat something immediately before the wedding, too, so I packed two

SHAWN LANGWELL

sandwiches and a soda. Then we were off to set up signs and get ready for the big day.

As the processional music started, the birds began to chirp, and a gentle breeze cooled our guests. Adele looked stunning as she made her way down the aisle. I felt like I was in a dream. Over 150 close friends and family showed up to celebrate. As we said our vows and prepared to exchange rings, Bobby reached into his pocket and looked worried. He turned to my friend Melton, who also fumbled in his pockets searching for the ring. I was concerned. *Are you fucking kidding me? They lost the ring,* I thought, trying to hide my irritation. Then Melton shrugged his shoulders and glanced to Ben. Ben to Kelly, all the way down the line, until they reached Seth. My youngest brother reached into his pocket, grinned, and then held up the ring. Then he passed it back up the line. Everyone laughed at the prank.

Adele and I placed the rings on each other's fingers, though I had to wet my finger because it wouldn't go on at first. We kissed and walked back down the aisle as husband and wife. After all the family photos, we all made our way back up the freeway to the reception at Peacock Gap. I felt so much love from everyone who was there.

Bill, our photographer, took some really great images of the party—everyone dancing, friends hanging out laughing, and my new bride and I smiling. The one shot that will forever be burned into my mind, though, was when I was on the patio that overlooked the driving range. I had my head down with one arm on the shoulder of my grandfather, and the other on my dad's shoulder. It meant so much to me that they were both there. I had not been with both of them together since I was eleven years old. Bill captured the moment on film—me in full ugly face as I sobbed tears of joy.

Everyone had a blast, and the next day we would be off to Kauai for our honeymoon. When we returned, we spent the next year trying to get pregnant. When that didn't work we decided to put that on hold and save up for a house instead.

God's Timing

Though we both really wanted to stay in Marin, we looked and looked and could not find anything that we could afford. So we started looking in Petaluma.

We both wanted a clean, quiet, safe neighborhood with good schools. After looking at several places over a couple weekends we finally found one we liked. Our agent, who was relatively new to real estate, presented our offer. It was accepted. We now had to come up with a down payment and get a loan.

Adele's aunt had promised to "help us with a down payment" when the time came. We had saved up about $8,000 and needed another $18,500 to close the deal. Her aunt cut us a check and said it was a loan, and that we could pay her back $75 a month. We were ecstatic. Thanks to my wife's help, we both had good credit and easily qualified for the loan to close the deal. In October of 1994, we became homeowners. It was a three bedroom, two and one-half bath, two-story home, with a large sunny backyard and indoor laundry. It was also in a quiet neighborhood, near good schools. There was a community pool and hot tub with low HOA dues.

The neighborhood became even better over the next several years, as a new shopping center, new junior high, a park, and a junior college were all built nearby.

In January, after an all-day ski trip, as soon as I walked in Adele smiled at me and said, "it's time." I was exhausted and we hadn't really talked about trying to get pregnant for a while but when it's time, it's time. She got pregnant that day.

While starting a family was something we both wanted, there were also some very real fears that surfaced when the pregnancy test came back positive. A few members of her family had medical issues that had the possibility of showing up in our unborn child. Her sister had been diagnosed with a bipolar disorder and her brother was born with cerebral palsy and is deaf. To assuage our anxiety, she had a series of tests done. The doctors concluded that there should be no cause for concern related to any potential hereditary issues. Regardless, we still discussed the "what ifs," and both agreed that no matter what, we would love the child and provide as best we could. We were not going to church, though she was raised Catholic, but we prayed anyway and trusted that all would be well. Of course we were flat broke and worried about food, day care, clothes, and all the usual. But friends came through and we always had enough.

All was going well until she started having pre-term contractions at seven and a half months. We feared that she'd miscarry. Her doctor ordered her to bed rest for the next six weeks. She was to take it easy and not do anything strenuous. In a subsequent follow up, it was determined that the baby was breached and that he wanted her to lay flat in bed, only getting up to eat, shower and use the restroom.

A couple weeks later, we were back at Marin General Hospital. We had an appointment to turn the baby manually in the hopes that she could deliver vaginally.

Adele was admitted and given a private room where we waited for the doctor to arrive.

The doctor was a kind man with a gentle bedside manner that put us at ease. He put some jelly on her belly and scanned with the ultrasound. You could see a tiny silhouette of our baby inside. The heart monitor beat steadily and made a loud whooshing sound.

"This won't hurt, but you will feel some pressure," he explained, pressing firmly on her abdomen in a counter-clockwise motion. After a few minutes he had successfully turned our baby head side down.

"That should be good," he said. "But, I want you to stay for a bit while we monitor you and the baby. I'll be back in an hour to see if we can send you home." We sighed in relief.

I pulled a chair alongside her bed so we could chat while we waited. She scooted up in her bed. As she did, I heard the heart monitor slow. My own heart dropped—I felt like the wind was knocked out of me. I had already been down this road with my grandmother a few years earlier. I didn't want to re-live this. Not now. Not with our unborn baby.

"Did you hear that?" I asked, heart pounding in my chest, worried about our baby.

"No. What?"

"When you moved, the baby's heart slowed," I said, pointing to the ultrasound.

"I didn't hear anything." Adele replied, shaking her head.

The baby's heart went back to normal as she sat still. My mind was reeling. I had a knot in my stomach.

"Do you think it's possible that the umbilical cord is pinched? Maybe it got wrapped around the baby's neck when the doctor turned it?" She looked at me like I was overreacting.

"I think its fine. He knows what he's doing," she said, not overly concerned.

"What if you go home and you bend over to pick up a bar of soap in the shower and the baby dies?" I worried. "Can you do me a favor—get out of bed and bend at the waist to touch your toes?"

"Fine," she said, rolling her eyes.

She sat up, and slid to the edge of the bed, got to her feet, and bent over to touch her toes. As soon as she did, an alarm screeched on the ultrasound—the baby's heart slowed to near flat line.

"Nurse!" I shouted, then turned to Adele. "Stand up and see if that helps."

As soon as she stood up, the baby's heart came back to a normal rhythm.

"Nurse, we need the doctor back here, now!"

I was climbing the walls, consumed by fear of losing our baby. The nurse arrived and we told her what happened. I demanded to get the doctor back.

Twenty minutes later, the doctor arrived. He concurred that the cord may be pinched and decided to do an emergency C-section. He explained everything in great detail, not at all rattled by the situation. He said that she and the baby would be fine, and that he needed to clear an OR and would get back to us shortly.

He returned and said we were scheduled for surgery in forty minutes. He explained that once Adele was prepped, the procedure would only take seven and a half minutes. In the meantime, he suggested we call her parents if they wanted to be here. I called and told Adele's parents what was going on. John and Phyllis lived nearby and showed up just before left for the OR.

I could see the fear on Adele's face. The clock ticked slowly as we waited. Finally, the doctor came to get us. Her expression softened, but I could still see the apprehension in Adele's eyes as he wheeled her off to surgery. As they left, the doctor told me to put on scrubs and a mask, and said the nurse would come get me in a couple minutes.

The nurse returned as he promised. Seven and a half minutes later, our son was born. He looked so tiny and wrinkled as the nurse help him up. I flashed a nervous smile, holding my breath as I waited for him to cry. Finally, after what seemed like an eternity, he let out a loud cry. Our son was alive! We were new parents. It was and is one of the happiest moments of my life. From the fear of possibly losing him to the pure joy of his first cry, I was overwhelmed with gratitude.

The nurse cleaned him up and wrapped him in a receiving blanket. I held him close to Adele's face.

"He smells so good!" she glowed, kissing our newborn son, Andrew, on the cheek.

I was beaming. I went to introduce Andrew to John and Phyllis. I handed Andrew to his grandma. Phyllis was always a strong woman. I never saw her cry. But as she held my son, she was overcome with joy, tears rolling off her pale cheeks. She then passed him to her husband. John beamed as he held Andrew carefully before handing him back to me.

I was so happy to be a dad, and I was fortunate to be able to take two weeks off to bond with our new son. He fit perfectly in the crook of my arm, and would fall asleep on my chest while I watched baseball. I could hardly wait for him to walk and play catch, and so much more. It was a challenge for my wife, though. She went back to work when Andrew was three months old. As any new parent knows, you don't sleep with a newborn in the house. There were many nights where she only got two to four hours of sleep a night.

Money was tight but we managed. After a first round of day care in Novato, which was not the best, my wife found the sweetest lady, who happened to live nearby, to watch our son while we were at work. She was one of the kindest women I knew. Linda was a thin elderly woman with flaming red hair and a thick Columbian accent. Every morning she greeted us with smile—sometimes with tired eyes.

"Como estas, mijo?" she'd ask my son, love in her eyes. "Tienes hambre?"

She watched several kids at once and spoiled the babies with home cooked baby food. She'd make them pureed sweet potatoes or carrots, mashed peas, or soft boiled eggs. It was a blessing to find her. My mom was also kind enough to come to watch him one or two days a week. They always had so much fun playing in the back yard or watching Disney movies, or Blue's Clues and that Purple Dinosaur, Barney. Andrew would also get to spend time with my in-laws, helping grandpa rake leaves or grandma go to the store when he got a little older.

The first few years of being a dad flew by. Even though I was on the road two to three times a year for work, I was fortunate to be there for nearly every one of my son's firsts.

Tee ball was one of those firsts. I watched as several kids stepped up to smack the ball off a tee. They were so excited when they hit the ball many took off running down the third base line. Pure joy. They didn't care, they were playing baseball. I also got to watch a lot of Barry Bonds and Giants Baseball with Andrew. There are fond memories when he and his friends sat in front of the TV chanting "Barry! Barry!" as Barry Bonds stepped up to smack another home run.

When Andrew was four, Seth came over to visit. I grinned as they kicked the soccer ball around in the backyard. Andrew laughed as he chased his uncle around, trying to steal the ball. Seth was eating it up, and decided to show Andrew a few tricks.

He dribbled right up to Andrew, taunting him to try and steal the ball. Andrew took the bait, and as soon as he tried to get the ball from his uncle, Seth pulled the ball back with his foot, then back kicked it twenty feet away before dribbling back toward Andrew.

As his uncle showed off, Andrew's eyes lit up. He was determined to steal the ball from his big uncle. Just as Andrew reached for the ball with his foot, Seth did a ball flip over his shoulder, kicked the ball against the fence, and ran around the yard with his hands in the air, yelling, "Goooal!"

Chapter 20
Kiss Your Babies

At 6:30 a.m. my alarm went off, just as it had every other weekday for the past six and a half years since I started working at Mix Magazine. The smell of coffee wafted up the stairwell. I scratched, rubbed my eyes, and made my way downstairs to grab a cup of coffee and go outside to have a smoke on the front porch—a routine that I started far too long ago. The hot coffee and nicotine rush got my motor humming—*breakfast of champions*, I thought.

Having a little quiet time in the morning was an important part of my day that helped me get centered and connect spiritually. Some days, though, it was just an excuse to smoke and have a cup of coffee as I dreamed of all the ways I was going to conquer and save the world. What a crock. I finished my smoke, washed my face and hands, and went to wake up my son up before he went to Linda's. When we got there, she welcomed us inside. She took Andrew's stuff and set it on the sofa before leading us to the kitchen table.

"Quieres juevos, hoy?" (Would you like eggs today?)

"Si! Me gusto mucho!" he said. (Yes, I like them very much!)

Today it was soft boiled eggs for breakfast. She had been his nanny for over four years. In the fall he would start pre-school.

I gave my son a hug and a kiss goodbye.

"Adios," I said to Linda and my son.

"Que te vayas bien," she replied. (May it go well for you)

My commute to Emeryville was over an hour and fifteen minutes each way. In the summer I could make it in an hour. In the winter it could take as much as two hours each way. It was a grind, but it was a good job.

I listened to the radio as I made my way down Highway 101 cruising in my red Toyota pick-up. I had bought it new from the lot in San Rafael that I used to walk by every day on my way to work at Dominic's in high school, dreaming of one day being able to walk onto the lot and buy a brand new car.

Though I still smoked, I had promised my wife I wouldn't smoke in the truck so my son wouldn't have to breathe it. Most days it was not a big deal, but sometimes I'd get to work so agitated from traffic and nicotine withdrawal, that I'd smoke two before going into the office.

Commuting in heavy traffic for 84 miles round trip every day wore me out. Road rage had become a growing problem in the Bay Area and around the country, and I was being tested nearly every day. I did my best not to instigate it. Instead, if I was too worked up, I'd yell and scream in the confines of my truck. That worked most of the time, but not always. I was one of those uptight drivers that cussed and yelled to myself, and flipped people off for cutting in front of me—not very serene or spiritual, to say the least. After several accidents, scaring the crap out of my wife, and getting sideswiped by a semi-truck, I eventually calmed down. Life is too short to get uptight behind the wheel.

Today, though, traffic was light. It was summer and school was out, which meant less traffic. I made it to work at 8:45 a.m.—just enough time to choke down two cigarettes before heading into work at 9:00 a.m.

Our offices were in the old Jelly Belly jelly bean factory in Emeryville. Huge skylights lined the ceiling and filled the whole space, including my office, with bright natural light.

I booted up my computer and went downstairs for a cup of coffee. Then I returned to my desk to check email and phone messages. The message indicator light was blank—no voice mail. I checked my email—there were five new messages.

I glanced at my emails, and responded to the first. The second came from the managing director of Abbey Road Studios, in London. I got excited—Abbey Road is a legendary studio where the Beatles recorded many of their albums in the sixties. I was thrilled, he had graciously accepted my offer to participate in a special supplement we were publishing—a calendar featuring *Great Recording Studios of the World.*

For some this may not seem like a very big deal. For me, it was. I had been given more and more opportunities over the past few years, forcing me to stretch far beyond my comfort zone. This project required me to cold call recording engineers, producers, managing directors, and studios owners of some of the most famous recording studios in the world. I emailed and would follow up by phone early in the morning or late at night to reach them in varied time zones.

I had never done anything like this before. I had little to no knowledge of the recording business, music industry or even selling advertising prior to working at this company.

Now I was cast into a position where the publisher coached me to believe that we had something our clients wanted and needed. All I had to do was make the contact, and sell the benefit. It worked. I think it worked because I believed in what we were selling. We were, according to many of our readers, the number one publication serving the professional sound and recording industry and were heavily involved and vested in serving our clients...I would go on to sell three other special publications including one that put me across the desk at some of the world's most famous sound stages and post production rooms: Disney, Warner Brothers, Paramount, and Twentieth century Fox, to name a few. In fact, for one of the special sections, I was to meet with the manager at Sony Music Studios in New York, but was told to leave the building because Michael Jackson was in the house.

I was blessed and grateful.

Many years later, I realized just how very important those early days were. Those projects gave me the confidence to realize that I could be successful once I pushed through my fear of rejection. It also helped when I had someone to encourage me and collaborate with. Freelance business writer, Dan Daley, was that guy on these projects and I used his influence to get the doors open and help close the deal. Thanks Dan.

I promptly drafted a reply. I was grinning so hard it hurt my face, as I hit send.

Then the phone rang.

"Shawn—Dave O 'Connor. Do you have a minute?" he asked in a serious tone.

My heart raced. *Why would he be calling me this early at work on a Wednesday?*

"Yeah, sure. What's up?"

"We lost your brother," he said directly, ripping the band aid right off.

"What?!"

"We lost your brother—Seth is gone."

I paused, trying to process what he just said.

"What?! What do you mean? Did he not come home?" I asked praying that's all he meant, but my gut said it was worse. I heard what he said but I was in shock.

"No. We lost him. He's dead...car accident..."

As he spoke, I felt my throat tighten, the air rushing out of me. "What happened?! How?" Then the reality of the situation hit me—*MY BROTHER IS DEAD!*

"No!" I cried. "No...I can't believe it." I lowered my head, placing my hand on my forehead, and sobbed into the phone. *My little brother was dead. Why? It's not fair...*I thought. *I should've spent more time with him, helped him get sober. But he was doing so good...*It was too late. He was gone.

"I'm so sorry," Dave said, maintaining his composure, choking back tears. "The sheriff just came by to let us know. You're mom is beside herself..."

"I can't believe it. How did it happen? Where? When?" I asked in rapid fire, hoping the answers would somehow make it easier to accept the grave news.

"Petaluma. According to the sheriff, he apparently fell asleep at the wheel on the way to work. There were witnesses—he swerved to avoid a flatbed, then drifted right off the road into the redwood trees just past East Washington

Avenue off Highway 101. They found him curled up in a ball on the passenger's side of the floor…. Beer cans were found in the back…. That's all I know for now. I'm so sorry, Shawn."

I sat up and wiped my cheeks, shaking my head in disbelief.

"Tell my mom I love her. I'll call later. Does Kelly know?"

"I'll call him and the rest of the family."

"Thank you," I said, trying to be strong. My brother was dead! My mind was reeling. David was very empathetic but business-like which helped me maintain a level of composure at work.

"What about Jonny? Does he know?"

"No. Do you want to call him? He was very close to your brother, I'll take care of all the rest."

"Yeah, I'll let him know."

As I hung up the phone, a tidal wave of grief overcame me. I sat with it. After a few minutes, I regained my composure, and then walked down the hall to let my boss know the bad news. She must have sensed my distress.

"What's the matter?" she asked.

"My brother's dead," I mumbled, trying to hold back the tears as best I could.

Her eyes welled up. She covered her mouth with both hands.

"Oh my God! I am so sorry. What happened?"

"Car crash—apparently he fell asleep at the wheel on his way to work early this morning."

I thought to myself there's more here and tried to make sense of what happened—I pictured his lifeless six-foot tall,

210 lb. body curled up in a fetal position on the passenger's side floor board of his purple 1989 VW bug, the beer cans, his struggle with his recovery—then, I quickly dismissed the thought. It didn't matter. He was gone.

"I'm shocked. I can't believe it. Why?! Why did he have to die so young?!" I said, burying my face in my hands.

"Oh Shawn, I'm so sorry. You need to go home to be with your family."

"I will. I need to call my wife and best friend first, okay?" I said, wiping the tears with my sleeve.

"Do what you need to. Let me know if you need help with anything," she said, biting her lip.

I returned to my office and decided to call Jonny first. He had been Seth's best friend. It was early for him—I'd probably wake him up. He was usually up until 2 or 3 a.m. every night.

I dialed. It rang three times.

"Hey. What's up?"

"Jonny, It's Shawn. Sorry to wake you up so early."

"No problem. What's up?"

"Seth's dead. He died in a car accident."

"Shut up! You're joking. "

"No. I wish it wasn't true. He's dead…. Jonny, my brother is dead!" I started sobbing.

"No way. Shut up. No. No way. Shut up. No. No. Shut the fuck up!"

"Jonny, I'm serious…he's gone." My voice cracked. "He's gone. Dude, I'm so sorry—he was your best friend."

"Yeah…he was, he's not dead. You're fucking kidding me…" he repeated, trying to deny the reality of the truth. My brother and Jonny's best friend was dead. "There's no way," he continued, "I just saw him the day before yesterday."

"I know. It totally sucks. I hadn't seen him in a while. He was going to help me dig fence posts, but he's gone. It's not fair!"

"No way! I CAN'T FUCKING BELIEVE IT!" he continued, still trying to come to grips with the grim reality that he in fact had just lost his best friend and roommate. He was no longer with us.

"Jonny, I'm so sorry dude. I've gotta call Adele and let her know. I'll call you later, k?"

"Okay. Dude, that fucking sucks!"

"Yes, it does. I'll call later, please let your sister know, too, and anyone else if you want."

I picked up the phone and called my wife. She, too, was in shock.

"Are you going to be okay?" she asked.

"Yeah, I'll be fine. I'm not going to drink or anything...I'm going home now."

"I love you," she said, "I'm so sorry. I'll be home soon, too."

"I love you, too."

I thought back to a few weeks earlier, when Seth had been over at our home showing our four-year-old son soccer tricks.

"When I grow up I want to kick a soccer ball like Uncle Seth," Andrew innocently told his mother and me one night after work.

There would be no more soccer lessons from his uncle; no more BBQs; no more funny off color jokes; no more bellowing laugh that was as contagious as my grandmother's; no more wide-eyed, flirty grins, or poems, or sweet nothings for his girlfriend; no more sticking up for his older brother at a bachelor party that got out of hand. He was gone. He had no more demons to battle or addictions to fight. At twenty-eight, two weeks before his twenty-ninth birthday, my baby brother was gone. I only pray that he is now popping wheelies in Heaven, smiling down on us.

In preparing to write this, I wanted some insight from both my mom and Dave to glean a little more from their perspective. We hadn't really talked about it much except around the holidays or each year on the anniversary of his death.

Mindful that it may open up old wounds, but necessary to have their perspective, I called my mom and let her know what my plans were, and I went over one afternoon and just listened.

My mom mentioned that she had said a prayer the day before my brother's death to release him into God's hands. "He doesn't have to fight anymore, Shawn—he doesn't have to fight," she said, voice wavering. He was now at peace.

To protect us all, Dave had insisted on being the one to identify him at the mortuary after the accident. With somber resolve Dave said, "That was the single most difficult thing I've ever had to do."

I looked at my mom. A wistful look in her eyes, she went back to that day, you could see it on her face. I was worried that it would be too painful, but she understood why I was doing this, and that it was healing.

She recalled, "It was early in the morning, the sheriff knocked, dogs barked...then..." I could see her eyes welling up, "Keening—I was keening, that guttural mournful cry...it started in my groin, up to my chest, then to my heart, and throat, and out my mouth. Asia (her neighbor) could hear it from across the street."

I got chills as she painted the picture of reliving the hardest day of her life. "He liked the sweet things—T&A," she continued. "As I drove down the street in the yellow Ford Courier, he'd reach over and hit the horn whenever I drove by a pretty girl. Please do him right. Honor him. Let the world know how kind he was."

"And don't forget to share his sense of humor," Dave added. "He always had a quick wit like no other."

"Of course, I will. I miss him. I love him. This is really for him and you."

Calling Dad

Later that first evening, I mustered the courage to call my dad to let him know Seth had died in a car crash.

"Oh no," he said in disbelief. He was clearly caught off guard, he sighed deeply, "Wow..."

"I'm so sorry, Dad." I expected more emotion from him; I wanted him to blubber and say how sorry he was that he didn't get to spend more time getting to know him. I wanted so much more.

"I'll let you know when the service is," I said, trying my best to not read more into my dad's stoic response to the tragic news.

"Okay. I love you, I'm sorry he's gone. Goodbye."

It was a brief call. I hung up the phone and went upstairs to cry my eyes out until my wife came home. I was crushed that my brother was gone, but talking with my dad and hearing how detached he sounded brought old resentments to the surface. I thought I had repaired my relationship with him years ago, and I now feared this would drive a wedge between us again.

On the other side, I will forever be grateful for my stepfather, Dave. He was our anchor in this process and wasted no time in trying to bring closure to a catastrophic loss. He took care of all the details, phone calls, all the hard stuff. He was a rock. Here's the obituary he placed in the Marin IJ:

Friday, June 18, 1999

Seth Adam Langwell
Accomplished Cyclist

Seth Adam Langwell, known by some as the "Wheelie King" for riding his bike on its rear wheel from Samuel Taylor Park to Fairfax with a police escort, died June 16 after a car accident in Petaluma. He was 28. Mr. Langwell lived for the past year in Novato, but he had previously lived in Woodacre, where he spent much of his youth. He graduated from Drake High School in 1988. He had been employed as a waiter and most recently was a journeyman plumber for a firm in Sonoma County. His interests included soccer, snowboarding, bicycling and poetry.

He is survived by his mother, Joan O'Connor of Forest Knolls; his father, Jim Langwell of Russian River; his girlfriend, Rene Fosdick of San Rafael; stepfather, David O'Connor; stepmother, Chris Langwell; three brothers,

Shawn of Petaluma, Kelly of Point Arena, and Tyler of Russian River; and his grandmother, Pauline Langwell of Nipomo.

Services will be held at 11 a.m. tomorrow at Roy's Redwoods in San Geronimo.

Memorial contributions can be made to Mothers Against Drunk Drivers.

* Reprinted with permission, *Marin Independent Journal*

Chapter 21
Through the Fire

The next evening I made chicken enchiladas for dinner—
one of the dishes my dad had taught me to make that was one
of our family favorites. After dinner, I helped my wife clean
up the kitchen and then went outside for an after dinner
smoke. I replayed my previous conversation with my dad and
tried to think of what to say when I called. I took a deep
breath, trying to set aside the pain and hurt of my broken
relationship with my father, and the grief of the current
situation, and dialed.

There had been aloofness in his voice when I first broke
the bad news to him two days earlier. *Stay focused. Don't pass
judgment*, I said to myself as the phone rang.

"Hello," my dad's wife, Chris, answered.

"Hi Chris, it's Shawn. Is my dad home?"

"Yeah. One sec. I'm so sorry about Seth," she offered,
sincerely.

"Thank you, me too. It just doesn't seem fair…"

"No…it's not…. Here, let me get your dad."

"Jim—Shawn's on the phone," she hollered to my dad.

"Be right there." I could hear him in the background; the
patio door squeaked open and clicked shut; their dog barked,
I could hear his footsteps drawing closer.

"Sh! Quiet Buster," Chris shushed their Irish Setter.

"Hello."

"Hi Dad. How are you holding up?"

"Fine," he said matter-of-factly. "How about you?"

"Not so good…" I sighed, feeling my throat tighten. "I just can't believe he's gone."

"I know, Son, but he's in a better place now," my dad said with love.

"Yeah, I guess he is…. So…the service is this Saturday—tomorrow, at Roy's Redwoods by the golf course at 11 a.m. Do you remember where that is?"

"I do—" he replied, followed by a long pause. "We're not going to be there."

"What?!" I couldn't believe what I'd heard. *Are you fucking kidding me?!*

"We won't be there," he repeated somberly.

"Seriously Dad?!" His words cut through me like a knife.

Wounds. Hurts. Some ran deep. No matter how hard we try to set aside the past, when it's not fully reconciled, situations may arise that unleash the fear, anger and resentment of the past. Like Medusa, anger rears its ugly head and, unwittingly, the scars of past, hurt, sorrow, or fear come rushing back. I cracked.

"I've made my peace," he said.

"Really, Dad?! Made your peace? He was your son—can't you at least pay your respects?!"

His words stung. All the hurt, pain, anger, and resentment of him leaving us without even saying goodbye twenty-two years earlier seethed inside me like a bubbling cauldron of toxic stew—I was livid. *Made your peace? What the hell did that mean?* It sounded like a cop-out to me—he was using religion as an escape. Sure, I had a "higher power" that had enabled me to get sober, but in the moment I hated God, I hated religion—*What kind of God would take a son? A brother? A friend? Why?*

I guess I had not yet fully forgiven my father from a long time ago…*five years of therapy…amends…all wasted,* I thought.

I had met with him several years earlier to make amends, which is one of the necessary steps of recovery to clean up the wreckage of an alcoholics past, and is all about changing attitude and behavior and finding forgiveness. I had never been so angry in my entire life.

"I don't believe it! How can you not even show up to your own son's funeral?!!" I continued with my spiteful tirade, "What kind of father are you?!"

"I've made my peace. I'm going to hang up," he said.

As I listened to his calm, unemotional matter-of-fact response, I lost it. I wanted him to be there. I wanted to hug him. Maybe he had found peace in his own way of grieving, but it wasn't what I wanted to hear. What came out of my mouth next was full of hate. I crossed the line into pure rage.

"HOW CAN YOU NOT EVEN SHOW UP TO HONOR YOUR DEAD SON?!" I dumped it all on him.

"FIRST YOU LEAVE US WITHOUT SAYING GOODBYE. NOW, WHEN ONE OF YOUR SONS IS DEAD, YOU DON'T EVEN HAVE THE COURAGE TO SAY GOODBYE….YOU'RE A YELLOW-BELLIED COWARD!!! I FUCKING HATE YOU!!!! HOW COULD YOU?!" I continued with my vengeful diatribe—"Is it because you're embarrassed about leaving us, and don't want to face all the people who you used to be friends with?"

"I've made my peace," he said again, calmly.

"I don't understand."

"I've made my peace. I'm sorry he's gone. But I don't need to be there."

"I can't believe it. I'm hurt," I said sharply. "I just can't believe that you don't want to be there for your son."

"I need to go—goodbye," he said with a solemn certitude that left me feeling abandoned all over again.

"Bye..." I was crushed. I didn't know how to respond. I slammed the phone down into the cradle with raw, unbridled rage. That wasn't enough—I was furious—really, I was hurt. I picked the phone back up and slammed it back down repeatedly. Cursing at the top of my lungs, my rage unleashed. I ripped the phone out of the wall and hurled it across the room, just missing my son.

"Oh my God!!!" my wife exclaimed. "Shawn, stop! I know it hurts. I can't believe it either, but you need to calm down. You're scaring us."

Realizing how close I came to hitting my son in the head with the phone, I dropped to my knees and bawled. I brought my knees up to my chest and rocked, trying to calm down.

"I just wanted to be loved. I just wanted to know he cared," I blubbered. I knew that he cared, but in that moment, all I could think about was how I was let down again. Was it too much to expect a parent to want to show up for his dead son's service?

In hindsight, after many years of therapy and practice, I would come to realize that I can't control people, places, or things. I wanted him there for selfish reasons, and was not at all empathetic of his needs, process, or grief; I expected my dad to show at least some modicum of remorse and concern—to comfort me, to make my pain go away, to save *me* from my own grief. The fact is, we can't control other people's emotions or reactions or behaviors, and no matter how badly I wanted my dad to rescue me, or, at least, to be there for me this time, I needed to accept that he was processing his grief in his own way—not my way, or the way I wanted.

We don't get to dictate how another should react in a given situation. Regardless, of what I wanted, or how I thought he should respond, I held onto an unrealistic expectation wrapped in fear. I somehow believed that all the pain from the broken relationship with my father would magically be erased and pull us together with the loss of my brother. That's what I wished for. It's what I expected. God had other plans.

In many years since my brother died, I have read several books that have been written about the stages of grief. Pain and loss and grief are such an emotional roller coaster. We all will experience the ride at some point in our lives. I didn't realize how tightly I still held onto the pain, anger and resentment surrounding my relationship with my dad.

Years later, I would take steps to look at my part and ask forgiveness—again, in an effort to make peace with my father.

Chapter 22
In God's Hands

On a brisk June morning I pulled alongside Nicasio Reservoir to write a few words about my brother. I found a quiet spot among the reeds, to be still and reflect. As I sat there, waves of emotion overcame me. Tears streamed down my gaunt face splashing on the college ruled pages of my notebook.

"God, help me!" I cried out, not caring if anyone else was around. "Why did you have to take my brother so soon?!"

A few blackbirds flew by chasing bugs for breakfast.

A gentle breeze dried the salty tears from my cheeks as I began to write. Not knowing where my words would go or what would hit the page, I just began to write, and write, and write. Reflecting on the short life of my youngest brother, a poem came to mind. Then grief punched me in the gut—I wailed aloud, "Why?! Why? Why?!!!"

I "dropped down to a heart level," as my sponsor would say. It's that place in our heart of hearts or soul where our spirit lives—pure love. The lump in my throat reminded me again of how tragic this loss was. I continued to fight through the grief, to pour my love for my brother onto tear-stained pages as best I could. I felt a duty to honor him.

Another gentle breeze kissed my cheeks, like a whisper from God....

"Keep going" were the words I heard in my head that inspired me to press on. For the next half hour I wrote, but it didn't feel like my words. I was just putting words to paper, and was in a zone that was so pure. I paused to read back over what I had just written. It was perfect.

The next day was the memorial at Roy's Redwoods in San Geronimo. I was blown away at how many cars were already lined up along Nicasio Valley Road. We parked and walked toward the meadow at Roy's Redwoods. It was sunny and starting to warm up.

At the foot of the trail, we ran into a longtime friend of the family, Marty. He offered his condolences to our family, and asked how I was doing. He asked if my dad was going to show up. They were friends for a while just before my dad left us. I explained how upset I was that my dad wasn't going to be at the funeral. Marty has been a family friend for a long time and was there for us when my dad left.

"You know," he said, "maybe that's the way it's supposed to be," he raised his eyebrows.

"Yeah, you're probably right. Thank you!" I hugged him while choking back the tears. "You're a good man, Marty...Thank you!"

With my wife's hand in my right and my son's in my left, we made our way to the far side of the meadow. As we approached, we were greeted by hundreds and hundreds of friends and family giving their love, condolences, and hugs.

"We're so sorry, Shawn."

"He's in a good place with his friend now," I replied.

My mom, Kelly, Dave, and nephew, Spencer, stood alongside a decaying redwood tree at the far end of the meadow. Its bark had long been stripped, and what remained was a smooth twenty-foot section marked with hearts and romantic teen carvings—"JT + KD" or "JS was here"—my mother buried her head into my shoulder and sobbed. "I know, Momma, it hurts. But he's not in pain anymore," I hugged her.

Though loved by many, in an attempt to love himself, Seth had his own demons to fight. He'd won several battles, but ultimately, he succumbed.

Several long term childhood friends of mine—Kevin, PJ, Joe, James, Antony, and many more, stood along the edge of the meadow under the shade of the towering redwoods. These were friends who, twenty-two years earlier, had made me feel welcomed after I had endured changing schools three times in four years prior to settling into the San Geronimo Valley. Now, each stood tall and offered their support for our family at my brother's memorial. They are friends for life—we're there for each other when we need help.

I wept, not so much out of sadness, rather from a sense of gratitude for those who showed up.

The breeze grew stronger. A couple of birds chirped. My heart opened up, and felt as if a huge light embraced us all.

Sensing Seth's spirit, I looked up. "Hi, Bro," I murmured. "Pretty cool, isn't it? Look how many people love you."

The words of my brother's spirit in response were clear as day, *"Yeah, you guys will be okay. Just do Mom right."* I smiled, looking to the sky. I wiped the tears from my face, and made my way back to the small family circle at the far end of the meadow.

Several friends, relatives, and extended family spoke, sharing stories and joyful memories of my brother and what he meant to them. All offered their condolences to the family. The mood was not somber, it was a true celebration of a life honoring my brother.

The Nuyen brothers sang a song. James and his brother, Mark, sang, too. Then my mom and Dave said a few words. When it was my turn, I began to read the eulogy that had come to me the morning before. As I began to read, I looked upon the meadow. And was overcome with a sense of gratitude. Over 400 people stood before me, there to celebrate Seth's life and pay their respects. It was a bit overwhelming. I paused and looked up. "God, please watch over him," I prayed aloud. A gentle breeze swayed the tops of the one hundred fifty foot tall redwoods encircling the massive meadow.

I *knew* Seth was there. I felt his presence in the soft breeze kissing the tops of the redwoods, and in the songs of the singing birds. I knew, then, he was at peace and smiling over us. I pictured him skydiving, saying, "Look Ma, no hands!" or riding an endless wheelie in Heaven, saying, "Don't forget me, I'm the Wheelie King...."

Quest for More

After Seth died, drinking was not an issue. Instead, I poured myself into my career. I continued to climb the invisible corporate ladder and made more money. Success and its trappings felt good, and I was mesmerized by the opportunity for more. It was nice to be one of the "haves" rather than a "have-nots" for a change—especially after many years of barely getting by. Our lifestyle was far from ostentatious, but our rise to upper-middle class enabled me to do things that before I could only dream of. We vacationed, bought a few toys, and made improvements to our home.

But, I wanted more. I wanted to be wealthy. Ever since my father left and finances were tight, I wanted to make it big. I wanted to have nice things and become independent. Though my mother had taught me how to take care of the necessities—how to survive—I had no real role models to show me how to pursue wealth nor achieve financial independence.

I sought out leaders—business men and women, and motivational speakers with an unquenchable desire to become successful. I read books and listened to many motivational speakers on tape who shared strategies on how to change the way I thought. These speakers shared tips on how to ask better questions, to change my own self-talk, and to build from the inside out. Many said that the key to success was found by helping others—that by doing so, I would enrich the lives of others and, in the process, earn more money.

I invested thousands of dollars and hours in pursuit of becoming rich and breaking free from the bondage of debt. Don't get me wrong, there is nothing wrong with money. We need it. I applaud effort, determination, and hard work. But back then, I lacked the proper training, perspective, and knowledge necessary to build any lasting wealth. In short, I continued to trade time for money. Becoming rich was my primary goal in life, and I was consumed by it. There were fleeting moments of huge spikes in my income that I wore like a badge of honor. The more I made, the more important

I felt. But, I also never forgot where I came from and was very generous.

Money filled the emptiness I felt inside. It made me feel powerful when I made more, and miserable when I was broke. In other words, my sense of identity was tied to my financial status. I started using credit to buy more things that I didn't need to impress people I didn't know—an expensive car, electronics, more home improvements, etc. But in my stubborn ambitious pursuit of creating a life of fame and fortune, my priorities got mixed up. I forgot to pay attention to the emotional needs of my spouse and, to some extent, my son. Ultimately, my selfish pursuit of *more* and lack of empathy for them drove a wedge between us.

In 2001, the horrific tragedy of 9/11 hit. Shortly after, I was downsized. This turned out to be a blessing in disguise. The company offered me a generous severance package and rehired me as an independent contractor, giving me a pocketful of cash, and the freedom and flexibility to be my own boss.

Over the past twelve years, Adele and I had been fortunate to go on several trips: Maui, Kauai, Cancun, Disneyworld with our son, Yosemite, Taos, New Mexico, a cruise to Ensenada and Catalina, and several other local camping trips.

In 2002, we planned a big trip to Belize for our ten year anniversary. I really wanted to scuba dive on the Belize Barrier Reef, the largest living reef in the western hemisphere. I invested in pre-certification training at a local dive shop in Marin, and planned to earn my open water certification in Belize.

Belize was stunning, with turquoise blue waters and white sand beaches, quaint local shops, and friendly locals who spoke English.

We had found a beachfront condo on Ambergris Caye with spectacular views of the Caribbean. Despite the diesel stench from the supply and waste barge that docked outside our room every morning, it was an awesome location. We shopped at the local store and made most of our meals in the condo as we had done on several previous vacations. But on this trip, something seemed off; we were in paradise, yet I didn't feel as connected as we once were—we slept in separate rooms and talked briefly about the growing chasm in our relationship. We chose to set it aside for the moment, after all, it was our ten year anniversary.

I was consumed with getting my open water PADI certification, and made reservations with a local outfit to go diving the second or third day of the trip. My wife had no desire to go out—previously she had a couple bad experiences in the ocean: many years earlier, she nearly drowned in San Francisco Bay, when she fell off a cigarette boat, and ten years earlier, on our honeymoon, we both nearly got swept out to sea by the powerful rip current when we had drifted too far off the edge of the reef on Ke'e beach on Kauai.

The next morning, I walked through the dry-dock training and boarded the thirty foot boat with four to five other divers. Our guide was a PADI Divemaster with thousands of hours of dive experience. The dive spot was on the other side of the Barrier Reef, but we had to wait for the right moment to cross. As the waves began to crash over a small break in the Barrier Reef, the captain accelerated at full speed sending the boat up and over the steep face of the wave, pitching us safely on the other side of the reef.

We put on our gear and descended to about twenty feet. The reef was teeming with life. Never before had I seen so many bright colorful fish—yellows, oranges, and bright purple sea sponges and coral. Our guide pointed to a Moray eel. Our group swam closer, watching as it gnashed his teeth, warning us to stay clear. We swam along the reef for a few minutes, soaking it all in. Then our guide pointed to a hole that was sixty feet deep, which would be where I would complete the final maneuvers to earn my open water PADI Scuba certification. He had instructed the others to stay nearby while we swam to the bottom to complete my final certification test.

He motioned for me to drop my weight belt, which I did, and then had me retrieve it and put it back on. Next, I had to properly demonstrate clearing my mask. No big deal, *right?*— except I kept screwing it up in the pool while training back home, and I was worried I'd screw it up again. Instead of holding my mask tight at the top and blowing though my nose to clear it, I accidentally pushed it up. My mask filled with saltwater, stinging my eyes. As I rushed to put the mask back on properly and clear it, I knocked the regulator out of my mouth. What was bad suddenly got worse. I panicked and choked on a big gulp of sea water. I fully inflated my BCD (Buoyancy Control Device—a vest that enables divers to float). Not a good idea at a depth of sixty feet—I'd pop to the surface like a champagne cork and likely get the bends and have to be sent to a decompression chamber all the way in Cancun. To avoid excessive nitrogen build up and to properly decompress and avoid getting the bends, I should ascend at a rate not to exceed sixty feet per minute. (According to PADI Dive Table General rules).

I was sure I was drowning. I saw my life flash before me. I pictured my son and thought about how much I loved him. I had to live for him and my wife. *I am not ready to go.* I prayed for God's mercy. Fortunately, my instructor was right there and quickly grabbed my vest, deflated it, and got my attention. To get me to focus, he pointed his two fingers to my eyes, then his. He then waved his hands to say, *slow down.* I would be okay.

Over the next minute, we slowly rose. I calmed down and stopped flailing. I had air. I was not going to die. After what seemed like an eternity, he safely guided me to the surface. As soon as I surfaced, I ripped off my mask and gasped. The boat was anchored in the shallows where I'd seen several nurse sharks lazily swimming, looking for free food just before I surfaced. Even though they are docile, after what I had just endured, I was on edge. I raced up the aluminum ladder, slipped out of my BCD, and went to the rail to hurl. Then, overcome by what had just happened, I dropped to my knees. I could have died. *Why did all this stuff happen to me?*

We finally made it back to shore and I couldn't wait to get back to my wife to tell her I loved her and how scared I was.

"All I could think about was you and Andrew and how I didn't want to die." She held me as I wept.

The next few years were a whirlwind. My contract with the magazine was not renewed. I was distraught. *Had I honestly done my best? Could I have done more? How did I get here, again?* All the old tapes of negativity around money, abandonment, and poverty ran through my head as I racked my brain for what to do. The easy thing would be to find work at a restaurant, but I didn't know where. I had never been unemployed for more than a week or two my whole life, and out of necessity, I had to find work quickly.

God sent me another angel. I was enjoying breakfast with my in-law, wife, and son at a local restaurant when I just happened to run into a former work colleague from Dominic's Restaurant. We were a fantastic team when we worked together back in high school. I explained my situation, and he mentioned that he was now the Food and Beverage Director at Oakmont Golf Club in Santa Rosa. He suggested I come by in March, and he'd put me to work. I found something in the interim, and two months later was working with him once again. A year later, he left and the board of directors of the club promoted me to Food and Beverage Manager. It was a good job and I made great money but worked long hours and was withering away inside and out, and had no time with my family.

Then, in the summer of 2003, my mother-in-law suddenly became severely ill, stressing my wife out with worry and adding more strain to our rocky relationship.

I was working on the Fourth of July when I got a call from my wife.

"My mom's not doing good," she said, her voice trembling. "I don't think she's going to make it. Can you come to the hospital?"

"Oh, no…I'm so sorry. Yes, I'm on my way." I quickly hung up the phone, told my bar manager I had to go, and raced to the hospital. My brother in-law and sister in-law had already come up earlier that week. My wife's brother was not able to get out in time.

Phyllis was a very kind-hearted woman who had sacrificed so much of her life for her children and her husband. Now she was dying. My wife took it very hard.

As the sun set over Mount Tam in the twilight hours my brother-in-law read her the last rites. We encircled her and fed her ice chips, and talked and loved on her. She was determined that her husband would promise to make sure everyone was taken care of. It was clear she wanted to let go.

"How much longer? I just want to go" she kept asking, pain in her eyes.

Through the window of her private room, the setting sun cast an amber glow above Mount Tam. I had been here seven years earlier with my grandmother and wasn't afraid. We all let her know how much we loved her and said our goodbyes.

What a blessing to be able to have closure. The nursing staff told us later that they wished more families did that. I held Phyllis' cool hand and leaned in to ask if she was ready to let go. I knew she was torn, not wanting to leave us. She had fought all her life. Holding her frail hand, I asked her to look out the window, and to let her eyes find the light.

"Look at the beautiful sunset God made for you," I said. With a wistful sadness in her eyes she turned to look. I reassured her that we were all there to say goodbye and that she would be fine. "We will see you again in Heaven. When you're ready, let yourself go into the light. We love you." I don't know where any of that came from, but it felt like the right thing to say. She stared into the fading light in the corner of the window for a brief moment, then quietly passed away.

Love, life, and loss. When we're in love everything seems rosy; we have a joy and zest for life that usually trumps everything else. Conversely, most of us don't relish having to deal with the tough stuff, especially death. Each of the experiences, though tough at the time, became blessings because they helped me learn to accept our mortality.

I am no longer afraid of death, but that doesn't make it any easier to deal with the emotions of losing those we love. I've learned to not take the time we have left for granted. Rather, I strive to lighten up and look for love and joy in the simple things of life.

Chapter 23
Surrender and Acceptance

After burning myself out at the golf club for another month, a new management company took over. The new General Manager and I were not able to see eye to eye—he wanted to cut my income by $25k/year, which was not acceptable to me, so I was let go.

I had to battle my own inner demons that, once again, said I was a failure. I had to level my pride and get beyond the shame that I was once a very successful salesman who supported his family, and now I was fighting to keep my marriage and house. I went through a series of other restaurant jobs to put food on the table including getting rehired at the Lark Creek Inn. This time, though, I thrived. I worked there for around a year, until 2007 when I applied to The Press Democrat for the third time. On the two previous times, I was told I didn't have enough experience. *Well duh*, I thought, *I was fresh out of school.* This time though I had ten years of advertising experience, though not in newspapers. I had to interview three times and sell myself like there was no tomorrow. Finally in April of 2007, I was hired.

Much like my career at Mix Magazine, I started small. But in a short amount of time, I was given great opportunities that helped me become very successful, even as I continued to overcome self-doubt.

My wife and I were not connecting anymore, and somewhere along the line, the love we shared was lost. We had grown more and more distant. Though we thought we could make it, we finally decided it would be best to separate. I met with our pastor for advice, but there was no hope for resolution. We sought out a mediator and began the process of a legal separation.

The hardest thing was letting our son know. I felt so ashamed that we let him down. I had failed to keep my promise to not divorce as my parents had. It was devastating. Reliving that moment, even now, is just too painful. It saddens me to no end that I let him down. I don't wish that on anyone.

Suffice it to say, our divorce was one of the most difficult, heart wrenching things I ever had to do. I was crushed that my wife and I could not reconcile. No blame—I had my part, she had hers. Fortunately it was an amicable separation and we both continued to share in the parenting of our son. We showed up to his concerts and baseball games and shared custody. I realized later that he had held out hope that we would be able to get back together; we had avoided the "D" word with him. I later apologized for not being clear.

J.J.K.

It had been five years since Phyllis passed, and John was never the quite same. He had a stroke shortly after, but was determined to regain his strength and worked his butt off with a physical therapist to do just that. Even after his stroke, he had managed on his own—he was too stubborn to ask for help.

Adele and I had chosen not to let John know that we were divorcing yet. We weren't ready to.

There was a lot of change going on. Though Adele and I were separated, we continued to live together while we sorted things out.

One day, Adele said she hadn't heard from her father in a while—he wasn't returning any of her calls. She was worried and concerned. Fearing the worst, she went by the house after work with a work colleague. She heard him moaning from the backdoor and called the paramedics. They broke into the house and took him to Marin General Hospital. It was estimated by his beard that he'd been down for three days.

Adele and I held out hope that he would bounce back as he did after his stroke, but he was very weak. After several visits to check in, his health deteriorated rapidly. He had to be fed from a tube but started aspirating. He was not getting any nourishment, beside the IV, and in a matter of two weeks, he was gone.

John was a remarkable man of great integrity. He served as a flight navigator of B-29 bombers in WWII and B-26 bombers during The Korean War. He was a man of faith, which literally saved his life. On one of the missions, his plane had taken numerous flak hits. One left a five inch hole in the fuselage, about fifteen inches behind his head. He later revealed that he had his head bowed in prayer and that flak blew out a hole where his head would have been.

He was a role model for doing the right thing. I respected him, and as the co-executor of his estate, I had a fiduciary responsibility to follow through with his wishes. Even though

Adele and I were getting a divorce, we made a decision that, under the circumstances, we would follow through with our commitment to him. He had told me several times in previous years that he always wanted to be buried at Arlington National Cemetery. We honored his wish and made arrangements for his funeral.

The earliest date we could get was mid-November between Veteran's Day and Thanksgiving.

In the interim, I put my nose to the grindstone at work. One day at work, I noticed an attractive brunette with a great smile in the Real Estate Department. Our eyes connected for a moment and she smiled.

"I'm Shawn," I said. "I don't believe we've met."

"I'm Crissi. Nice to meet you."

"Likewise."

I smiled again, and turned to ask one of my colleagues who sat opposite her a question about a client, then went about my business. Shortly afterward, she was moved to the page layout department, and was now responsible for placing the ads in the paper. In other words, she was now working directly with advertising, so when I had to beg for a late ad to be placed, I would go to her. She was always so sweet and accommodating, even if the other reps or I were making her job more difficult. I kept all our interactions professional and only talked about business.

Several weeks went by and my assistant tried to play matchmaker. She kept trying to set me up on a blind date with one of her friends; she knew I was going through a divorce but I wasn't ready to date.

"It's just a date," she said.

"That's okay, I'm fine."

"Dude, you're a catch, and I have friends who would love to go out with a guy like you."

"Thanks, but not now," I politely refused.

I had recently been given a new territory and was determined to do well. Work was a good distraction. Plus, as co-executor of my ex-father in law's estate, I was meeting with estate attorneys and dealing with inheritance headaches while helping my ex clear out her father's house. I was getting paid for it, but it became overwhelming. Adele felt the same, and finally decided it would be best to let professionals handle the rest of the details. It was her call and I agreed.

"You know, Crissi likes you," my matchmaking assistant said one day, giving me a knowing look.

"Really?"

"Yeah—really."

Over the past month or so, I had been thinking more and more about Crissi. Even though we interacted only occasionally, I couldn't get her out of my mind. She was sweet, charming, attractive, and I sensed that she liked me, too. *What was I afraid of? What was holding me back?* I was still reeling from my pending divorce. I didn't want to get hurt again. My heart had become guarded, calloused, and jaded, and I was not yet willing to let anyone in again.

I wanted to ask her out, but kept making excuses: *How could I date someone at work? What would others think? What if we started dating and it didn't work out, and we still had to work together? What if....?*

Those two words are such a buzz-kill, that keep us locked in perpetual fear and paralyzing us from being bold enough take chances.

If we buy into them for any length of time we risk missing out on the potential joy and exhilaration what might be something wonderful. True living, I have found, happens when we take a deep breath, walk through our fear, have ten seconds of boldness, and ask the question...

"So...what are you doing this weekend?" I asked really fast, totally worried that she might have plans...

"Nothing...absolutely nothing!" she smiled. I got the hint.

"So you want to go out to lunch this weekend?" I asked, my heart pounding. It felt like I was back in high school, working up the courage to ask a girl to prom.

"Absolutely! I thought you'd never ask," she giggled.

"Where would you like to go?"

"How about the Russian River Brewing Company?"

"Can I pick you up at 11:30?"

"That's perfect."

I got her address and said goodnight.

The next day couldn't arrive soon enough. Of course, that night I agonized over all the what ifs and finally resigned myself to just go with the flow.

I picked her up at her house and then went to lunch.

It was a warm fall day in November. We sat on the patio and enjoyed a delicious pizza and got to know each other. An attractive younger woman sat two tables away, reading but within earshot of our first date conversation.

Crissi told me about her kids and how she came to be on her own. She had always wanted to work for the local paper and was now on the way to living her dream. I told her a little about my family and how I had wanted to work at the paper for the longest time, too—but, for some reason, it wasn't meant to be until recently. *Was she the reason I was not supposed to work there until now?*

Before the check came, I excused myself to use the restroom and pay the bill.

There are angels everywhere. I later found out when I was away, the young woman on the patio moved closer to chat with Crissi. She had asked her how long we were dating. Crissi said that we weren't dating, that we were just friends.

"Oh honey, he's into you…he went to go pay," the young woman told Crissi.

After lunch I led Crissi to a bench nearby. I looked at her and said, "there's something I've been dying to do." I leaned forward and kissed her.

It was a great first date—awkward at first, but we hit it off. The conversation felt natural and not forced. We enjoyed each other's company, and she was super easy to talk to. I was smitten, even though it was just a first date. Her sweet giggle made me feel light and happy.

I liked Crissi but it was too soon to say we were "dating." Besides, I was going to Washington D.C. the following Monday with Adele and her family for John's funeral; and the following week Crissi would be going to Disneyland for her thirty-first birthday.

For now, Crissi and I said goodbye, knowing we'd talk and text a few times over the next couple weeks.

Two days later I was on a plane to D.C. with my son and Adele. We had been on a many trips before, but this was the last, and it was just plain weird. We all flew from various parts of the country for the funeral—Adele, Andrew, and me from San Francisco; his other daughter, Michelle, her husband, Jeff, and their son, Nicoli from Santa Maria; his son, Jimmy and Jimmy's caretaker, Patricia, from Texas; and Jeff's mother, Paulette from Tennessee. There were a few other relatives that met us there who were from Baltimore.

Since we needed to be there for a couple of days anyway, we took the opportunity to visit a few of the landmarks and museums in Washington D.C. We saw the Lincoln Memorial, the White House, the Washington Monument and a couple of the museums along the National Mall, including the Air and Space Museum, Museum of Natural History, and the Holocaust Museum. All were interesting but the Holocaust Museum left me angry and sad for all genocide victims in the gas chambers in Auschwitz and Killing Fields of the Khmer Rouge in Cambodia. The sight and smell of four thousand victims shoes will be forever burned into my memory.

The next day was John's funeral.

To go from the Holocaust Museum one day to Arlington National Cemetery the next was like being put in the emotional spin cycle of American history. I stood before acres and acres of white tombstones that dotted the verdant hillsides like rows of dominoes, each representing the life of a soldier, or a family member of the departed soldiers who had served their country well.

War kills. The aftermath leaves a wake of pain for those left behind. All politics and ideology aside, I owe a debt of gratitude to all those who have fought and served to protect our freedom. We were there to honor a man who fulfilled his duty to his country and family. It was the right thing to do.

His casket was draped with the American flag and loaded on the back of a horse drawn carriage that followed a team of uniformed soldiers, as they marched to the funeral site.

A Firing Party stood ready behind the chaplain. The chaplain gave his benediction, and as he finished, a bugler standing to his right raised his silver trumpet and played "Taps." Each note pierced my heart like flaming arrow, commanding our attention and respect in remembrance for every life sacrificed for our freedom. "Taps" was immediately followed by the concussive rapport of three rifle shots from seven soldiers that echoed though the still November air. "Aim—Fire." *Chills.* "Aim—Fire." The shots echoed for an eternity. "Aim—Fire."

Then an officer presented the flag to Jimmy, John's only son. Jimmy glanced at it for a moment then passed it to Andrew.

Rest in peace John. Thank you for teaching me how to be a gentleman. "Job well done."

Acceptance

Learning to accept things as they are is a perpetual inner battle; *Is it okay if I make a mistake? What will people think of me? Am I a failure because my marriage fell apart?* All these self-deprecating thoughts raced through my mind in the weeks and months ahead. The challenge I continue to face, though, is how to actually accept it when bad things happen to good people or good things happen to bad people. The simple answer is, I just do. Like my former work colleague, Michelle, used to say when something didn't pan out the way we wanted at work, "it is what it is." There is wisdom in letting go; there is freedom in surrender. It sounds counter-intuitive. When we are faced with challenges, we want to fight. But sometimes what we need to do instead is relinquish our attempt to fix, solve, or extricate ourselves from an undesirable situation. For example, when I was caught in the rip current on Ke'e beach, I got lucky. I swam like crazy to get Adele and I safely back to the reef; I fought the current with all my strength and barely made it. I have a friend who was caught in the same rip current with his daughter. Even though he wanted to swim against the powerful current, he knew that the right thing to do was to go deeper—to swim out toward the open ocean, then swim parallel to the beach to escape the powerful rip current.

How about boogie boarding or surfing? When you are in the crash zone, that area where the waves are breaking, the right thing to do is not to try and catch the wave, or jump over it. Rather, it is best to dive under or through it. How about a fighter pilot caught in a tailspin? Intuition would say you need to grip the stick to pull back as hard as you can to pull out of the dive, however, in an over-generalized approach, the pilot "sticks the spin," meaning they turn into the direction of the spin in an effort to regain control of the aircraft. So it is with things that are uncomfortable; merely sweeping them away or avoiding them, or even pretending they don't exist does not remove the problem. Sometimes we have to face our fears, demons, or problems head on; we need to relinquish control; to ask for help or pray, or ask forgiveness. When we do, the spinning usually stops.

I believe that our faults and failures are a part of a journey to get to where God wants us. Every moment of everyday, we are faced with a myriad of choices. We have been given free will to choose our path. Sometimes that road has a fork in it and we are faced with another decision.

Chapter 24
Love and Forgiveness

I awoke with a start one morning with a message powerfully etched on my heart and mind.

"You need to write about me. You need to tell our story." It was the voice of my brother, Seth. "Take them on a ride— my ride—our ride. Tell the truth. Let them know I love them, tell them I am free at last, and never, ever let them forget my name—The Wheelie King."

My dream came on the heels of a private message I had received on Facebook a week earlier from my brothers old girlfriend, Rene. She had come across one of Seth's old notebooks and wanted to know if I'd like them. Of course I said yes. I gave her my address and a few days later a packaged arrived.

Inside were a few of his poems, and some step-work and journal writing he'd done in early recovery. I have included a few excepts in his words. He would've wanted it that way.

On Sept. 25, 1996, as part of his step work, he wrote a piece called "Feelings of Anger Towards My Father":

I am upset that he left when I was so young that he never got to know who he really was and what he was all about.

Mad that I never had a dad to play catch or do father/ son things.

Angry that I had no father to look up to when I needed a dad.

Two days later, Seth wrote about "Forgiveness." One question in particular caught my attention, because I shared his struggle:

Who suffers when you refuse to forgive someone?

You suffer, he wrote. *Because if you don't forgive you can never be forgiven and also you suffer mentally, physically, and over a period of my life the patterns are a result of not forgiving.*

It's been said that the opposite of forgiveness is resentment. Seth and I shared resentment toward our dad and we both struggled with forgiveness.

Seth also wrote about the emptiness—the hole inside, that many of us have that needs to be filled with something—drugs, alcohol, food, sex, or _____. Fill in the blank.

For many of us the hole is the need to be recognized, loved or accepted.

It has been my experience that it is a "God-sized" hole that is only filled by grace, love, faith and forgiveness—spirituality, or a belief in a "higher power."

Reading through my brother's notebook rekindled the joy I had for my brother. It also brought up my unresolved grief over his death that I had buried deep in my heart for the past fifteen years. As I read though his private thoughts and feelings, I came to the slow realization that I had not fully grieved his death; that I was still holding on to lots of pain from my past that needed to be processed—that needed to be written about and, most importantly, needed to be let go of.

My brother and I shared similar feelings of fear, anger and resentment around my father abandoning us. I was Seth's father figure for a brief period after my dad left. I was only twelve-years-old and was responsible for keeping an eye on my baby brother.

This random notebook and the dream that ensued fueled my desire and need to write this story. I don't think my brother ever fully forgave himself or my dad. In many respects, his unresolved pain led to his battle with booze and drugs—a battle he fought valiantly, but ultimately lost.

In several conversations with friends as well as seeing, hearing and witnessing the lives of others, I see that every one of us has a story waiting to be told—one of joy and love but also episodes of deep-rooted pain, guilt, anger, regrets and shame—things that have kept us locked in our own prison. Some is stuffed so far down, like mine, that we sometimes don't even realize that we are still affected by not dealing with it by not letting go. Letting go is a far easier thing to talk about than to actually do. I thank my brother every day for his brutal honesty on paper. His notes reminded me that behind our pain and suffering and loss, are the seeds of joy— pure joy.

Granted, there are some hurts that one may never, ever want to forgive. Forgiveness doesn't change what happened, or exonerate one who's wronged us. In a simplistic sense, forgiveness is merely is an attitude and a conscious action to mentally, physically and spiritually let go of that which has caused fear, anger and resentment .

Through working the 12 steps, I came to realize that I could become free not only from drugs and alcohol but also of all that has held me back. By learning to forgive and be forgiven, I became free from the bondage of self; free to love; free to live. It didn't happen overnight. It took a lot of honest self-reflection, soul searching, prayer, and willingness to change my way of thinking.

In order to stay sober and maintain a healthy way of thinking, I need to practice working the steps and intentionally maintain a connection to God or my higher power on daily basis.

Each morning, I spend some time in prayer and meditation. The purpose is to set the stage for when I awake I ask God (my higher power), to direct my thinking for the day. There are a few prayers I read to get my mind focused on serving others. This keeps me out of selfishness and self-centeredness. I say the Serenity Prayer throughout the day, and do my best to be kind, patient, loving, and understanding towards those I interact with. Sometimes I mess up. Sometimes people piss me off. That's normal.

It was suggested a long time ago to never go to bed angry. I take an inventory of the day before my head hits the pillow. I ask God for forgiveness and to direct my thoughts and actions to do better next time. That is what it's about—to not let the things I've said or done that harmed another fester like an ingrown toenail.

Over the years I have learned to look at my part in a given situation, to learn from my mistakes, to humble myself, to admit it when I am wrong, and then apologize and ask for forgiveness. The point is, it's all about *progress not perfection*; ultimately *it's about a change of heart and love.*

Dave O'Connor

"Hey guess what? I've finally started writing a book," I mentioned to my stepdad.

"No kidding. What's it about?" Dave asked. He turned to me, and I could see he sincerely wanted to hear more.

"Forgiveness," I stated with a smile.

"You're shitting me!?" he said.

"No, I'm dead serious. It's something I've wanted to do for a long time, and I think the world could use a little forgiveness," I smiled.

"Ha!" my stepfather laughed, nodding his head in agreement. "You bet it does! Just the other day I was talking with some friends at church, and we were discussing how important and needed a series on forgiveness would be."

"Seriously?" I asked.

"Yeah, the world is crying out for it. Think how important and how many lives could be changed. Hell, you could change the world!"

"I wouldn't go that far," I chuckled.

"So how did you come about it?" he asked.

"I've spent my entire life battling resentment, fear, anxiety, addiction...you name it."

"Go on," he said, a knowing smile growing in his expression.

"I see others struggling with pain from their past, whatever that is. I held onto my anger around my dad leaving for a long time. I used it as an excuse to drink. When I worked my steps and learned to forgive, the pain began to dissipate."

He nodded, urging me to continue.

"There's a common saying that we are only as sick as our secrets. There's a couple steps that help us deal with those. One required me to write out a list of all my faults, how it affected me, and then take a hard look at my part in each of those different situations. The next one, required me to actually share all that junk with another person."

"Like a confessional?"

"Yeah, I guess so. After I did this with my sponsor I felt like I'd dropped a ton of bricks off my back. In the process I got sober, but I learned some great tools to change the way I think. Ultimately. I learned how to forgive myself and others."

He smiled. "I can't wait to read it."

Can We Forgive and Be Forgiven?

I had a conversation recently with my good friend, Jon. Years ago, we had mourned the death of my brother and his best friend. Now he is one of my best friends.

On this day, we were sitting in his car waiting for my son who had just qualified for the NorCal Junior College Regional Track and Field Finals in the 1500M with a time of 4:04.99. I was telling him about this book and we started talking about forgiveness.

He asked me, "If someone killed a member of your family, would you forgive them? Because if something happened to you or your family, I'm not lying, I couldn't forgive them."

I paused, while I thought of a response.

"It's not right, but my first thought is that I'd want justice. Like any convicted murderer—an eye for an eye. The problem is, that only perpetuates a never-ending cycle of anger and hate. But as a Christian, the other side of me knows that forgiveness and love are the answer."

"Why?" he asked.

Because if I don't forgive them, then I am allowing what that person did to keep me in a prison of anger and hate for the rest of my life.

"Basically, I am giving them free rent in my head, and the pain they caused will never go away as long as I hold on to anger and resentment. As you know those things will kill us. So the only answer is to forgive."

"Yeah, but I'm sorry, I couldn't do it. No way," he said, shaking his head.

"To each their own. When I look back at how angry I was and how long I held a resentment against my dad for letting me have drugs and for abandoning his family, I couldn't deal with the feelings. I smoked weed and drank and did drugs to escape from my feelings. My resentment and unwillingness to forgive him nearly cost me my life. He had "made peace" with the situation in his own way. But by holding a grudge for most of my life, it only hurt me more. Does that make sense?"

"Yeah, but that's different. Nobody was murdered or raped."

"True, but forgiveness is not selective. There's no measuring stick for what is forgivable and what is not. To be free, you need to forgive. Period. I know it sounds so counterintuitive, but why do you think this world is so fucked up? Why is there so much hate? In my opinion, it's because there are so many people hurting with deep wounds inside that have not been forgiven. I have had to ask forgiveness many, many times for the things I have said, thought, or done. As an alcoholic who has recovered from my addiction, it is a requirement for me to ask for forgiveness when I am wrong and to forgive those who have wronged me."

"I get it. But lying, stealing, or having your dad leave isn't the same as rape or murder."

"No, it's not. But think of it this way, resentment is like a cancer—it's unseen and slowly eats away at your joy. It causes bitterness and anger. It festers beneath your skin. Left unrecognized and untreated, it can swell, causing a pus filled cyst that eventually pops. Or it's like undetected cancer, that metastasizes and unexpectedly takes one's life."

"I still don't think they're the same," he insisted.

"Fair enough. I know that sounds a little extreme but there are plenty of studies to substantiate the impact that negative emotions like fear, anger and resentment have on our mental, physical, and spiritual health—they are not healthy."

"I just couldn't do it. I'm just saying."

"I know. You are not alone. I didn't think I'd ever be free from the anger around my dad. In fact, even after five years of therapy, making amends with him and asking his forgiveness for all the anger I held toward him, and him asking me to forgive him for all the things he did, it wasn't like a magic eraser washed away all the hurt and pain. I forgave, but I never forgot. It helped, but there were situations that would come up again several times—triggers—that brought back all those raw emotions from the past. Over time, I came to understand that forgiveness is a process, and that I would have to forgive again and again, every time the anger or uneasy feelings resurfaced.

"Hey," my son said as he walked up to the car. We had just watched him get a new personal record for the 1500 Meters at his track meet, before heading to the Giants game for my birthday. "What's up?"

"Were just having a deep conversation about resentment and forgiveness," I said.

"Cool. I'm ready to go to the Giants game."

Chapter 25
Second Chances

"If one advances confidently in the direction of his dreams, and endeavors to live the life which he has imagined, he will meet with a success unexpected in common hours."
—Henry David Thoreau

Have you ever heard the starfish story?

There was an old man who liked to go to the ocean to write. The salty air was an elixir for his soul and helped clear his mind. One day on a morning stroll along the water's edge, he could see a figure in the distance moving like a dancer. As he moved closer, he noticed a young boy picking up and tossing starfish back into the ocean, one after another.

"What are you doing, Son?"

"I'm saving the starfish," the boy replied with a proud smile.

"Well that's very good of you, Son, but they are probably already dead. What difference will it make?"

"What if it's not too late?" the boy asked. He picked up another, feeling its sandpaper-like arm twitch in his tiny hands.

He looked at the old man, "See. It's not too late for this one. It moved. It's alive!"

And with a big grin, he flung it as far as he could back into the surf.

*Adapted from a 16-page essay by Loren Eiseley, published in 1969 in the *Unexpected Universe*.

In hindsight, I realize that God always gives us an out and has other plans for us. It's never too late for a second chance. After I returned from the East Coast, my relationship with Crissi heated up. Because we didn't know how our supervisors would take it, we kept our relationship a secret at work for nearly four months before we were finally ready to let our co-workers know we were a couple. It was so fun, keeping it a secret at work. I think plenty of people knew, but it made our courtship even more exciting.

I invited her to meet my family at Thanksgiving—both my mom and stepfather adored her.

Yeah, I thought, *I have their approval.* Then it was my turn to meet her family at Christmas.

"Oh, come on over," she said. "There will be a few people there." When I walked in, there were more than thirty of her closest relatives. *Oh no, what am I getting into,* I thought. I met her parents, Gary and Nancy, two sisters, Heather and Melissa, and aunts and uncles, nieces and nephews, and her Grandma Elsie, whose warm smile immediately made me feel at ease. I could tell that she paid attention to everything. Grandmas are like that. Crissi's whole family welcomed me, and were just the right amount of crazy and real for me. I felt at home.

Those early days of courting were filled with lots of kisses and cuddles and being completely smitten. I got to meet her kids, which was admittedly awkward at first. They were nearly eleven and eight, and my son was thirteen. While I was busy at work and being a single dad, I spent virtually every weekend with Crissi and her kids. I know the kids hated having to give up their weekends to stay at my house to at first, but we managed to make it work.

Amidst all the change going on in my life—processing the emotions of finalizing a divorce, falling in love with a woman who loved me unconditionally, and being a dad for my teenage son, I was awarded Employee of the Year by our parent company, The New York Times Regional Media Group and Salesman of the Year from The Press Democrat. It caught me completely by surprise. I was just doing my job.

My mom had instilled a solid work ethic in me at an early age and was always there to encourage and support me with the choices I made. In early recovery, she wrote me a poem that has carried me through tough times over the years:

> *Life is serious.*
> *Life is fun.*
> *In many ways you've just begun,*
> *Sometimes we stumble,*
> *Sometimes we fall,*
> *Even when backed against a wall,*
> *Remember always when in your plight,*
> *At the end of the tunnel there is always light.*
> -Joan O' Connor, 1986

This poem has become a powerful reminder for me to push though the tough stuff; to remember to lighten up when I'm taking myself or a situation too seriously; to have hope for that which is yet unseen; to try again and again and let it be okay when I fall down; to get off the pity pot and back into the game. That, if you want the honest to God truth, is the primary purpose of this book—to walk through life's challenges and know that it's okay to make a mistake. We can learn to change—we can forgive. In so doing, we become free of the chains that bind us: fear, guilt, shame, inadequacy, pain. When we change our thinking, we learn to lighten up, forgive, and learn to love ourselves and others. It's not about me and all the crap that I've been through. It's about how love and faith truly are omnipotent. It's about the heart and soul of what it means to be human, to tap into that inner sprit inside each and every one of us that cries out, "I just want to be loved; to be told I am enough; to be told that it'll all be okay."

Unexpected Kindness

Crissi had her share of hardship. In particular, she was a single mother raising her kids on one income. She also held a lot of pride for doing things on her own. Having been raised by a single mom through my teen years, I could empathize with her challenges. I understood her need for independence. I understood what it was like to make do with what you had. I, too, was a single parent, and money was tight for both of us. This made it even more special when we had reason to celebrate. We went to dinner for my birthday and she handed me a beautiful handwritten card and a small paper sack. I didn't expect much. I reached inside and pulled out a small package wrapped in gold ribbon. Inside were tickets to "Wicked" and two nights at the Fairmont Hotel in San

Francisco. I was speechless, wiping the tears away, I said, "Thank you!"

"You are worth it," she said. "I love you and can't wait to spend a weekend with you!"

That's the kind of woman she is. We had a blast. The room was stunning. It had a monstrous tiled bathroom with fancy faucets and a glass shower. The bedding was soft and fluffy and inviting. There was even a winged chair with a small table to sit and read the paper while we snacked on brie and crackers. For the weekend, we felt like royalty.

The morning after our first night, we sat at a bistro table, sipping coffee outside a corner café, gazing upon the San Francisco Bay and Alcatraz, and feeling blessed beyond belief. That weekend Crissi made me feel special.

However, inside I was still guarded, and somewhat cautious. I fought off my inner trepidation of being closer to her. After all, I had just ended a marriage of sixteen years. I was thinking too much instead of just being present. Crissi's kindness and unconditional love drew me closer and made it easier for me to let go of my past and to love her. As our relationship grew, we began to dream of a life together.

On the dresser beside her bed she had a Post It note. It was an affirmation that said she was a published novelist, and had made the New York Times Best Seller list. She had always wanted to write a book, but never did it. I encouraged her to follow her dream. Then, one day, she decided to start. In a matter of a month she had her first rough draft.

In the interim, we had found and fallen in love with a secret weekend getaway in the hills above Middletown. It was a place where we could unplug, recharge and let the natural mineral hot springs restore us to mental, physical and spiritual health. Over the course of the next couple of years we went back to refresh at least every couple months. One cold afternoon while sitting by the fire, at the springs, I read through her first manuscript. It was a poignant tale of a young woman facing the challenge of being a single teenage mother. As I read the story, I was so proud of her. Years later, this book would be published as *A Road to Hope*.

In the summer of 2009, we went camping at the Cloverdale KOA. It was our first family trip with all three kids and us. It was a blast to watch the kids get to know each other better. That place is awesome. Our site overlooked hundreds of acres of vineyards in the Alexander Valley below. There were also cabins, a pool, and even a miniature golf course.

Over the next couple years, we spent time a lot of time together. There were days at the beach and pool, trips to Giants games, a visit to the Japanese Tea Gardens in Golden Gate Park, and a tour of Alcatraz with Crissi's family.

In 2010 I got my wish and the Giants finally won the World Series. It was a sign of more good to come. Crissi and I were getting serious and made the decision to merge households.

In April of 2011, she and the kids packed up and moved into my home in Petaluma.

At first it was not okay with her kids. My son was pissed too, because I had once told him I would wait until he graduated high school before combining households.

Over the next few months, Crissi and I knew we were meant to be together. Despite the challenges of merging households and seeing eye to eye in terms of parenting a blended family, our love for each other dictated that we would "figure it out." In August, we spent a week in San Diego for her sister, Melissa's wedding. In between planning and preparation for Melissa and Brian's wedding, we found time to boogie board and sunbathe at the beaches in San Diego.

In October I kept a promise to take the whole family to Disneyland. That was so much fun. I hadn't been since I was eight.

Some time that fall, I told Crissi's parents how crazy I was about their daughter and expressed my intent to propose. When I asked her dad for his blessing, he said, "Why are you asking me." I took that as a yes. We picked out rings and had them sized, but didn't know when they would be ready. We had planned a getaway to our secret spot in the hills, and she was really hoping that I would have the ring to officially propose. So she wouldn't be disappointed, I let her know that as much as I would love to, the ring was not ready yet. She was bummed, but we went anyway.

We made our way up the hill above Calistoga Ridge and found our favorite camping site along the small creek. After setting up the tent, we took the trail to the mineral pools to soak. Just before the pools is a bench that overlooks the Calistoga Valley, and is a spectacular spot to watch the sun rise or gaze at the full moon. It was midday, and I was hot and sweaty.

"Hold up," I said as I set my backpack down to tie my shoe.

Two young women sat at the edge of the cliff nearby, gazing at the valley below.

I pulled out a small box and on one knee, opened it. She clasped her hands over her mouth, realizing what was about to happen.

Looking up at her, "Crissi, we've been talking about this for a while," I said, fighting the lump in my throat. "I want to spend the rest of my life with you. Will you be my wife?"

"Here? Now?" she exclaimed, her hands shaking. I slipped the ring on her finger, and then pulled her into a kiss.

"Oh my God, I love you."

"Well, is that a yes?"

"You know the answer already. Of course!"

Over the next year, we planned and put it all together for a very special day, we changed our minds about menu and style a few times. We stressed about tiny details. In the end, it was perfect.

My old friend, Duane, and I set up the signs and balloons the morning of the wedding. I pulled the balloons out of the back seat to tie to the sign, when, "Someone Like You," by Adele, blasted on the stereo. A huge gust of wind came up and nearly blew the balloons out of my hand. I was overcome with a sense of God's presence and pure joy in the moment. It was indescribable. I knew this was meant to be. There are no accidents, no mistakes. This place, this woman, this family, even having my friend Duane there to help me—it was exactly as it was supposed to be. I felt all the hurt of my previous shattered love wash away with the wind, and I dropped to my knees to thank God for blessing me with so much—for blessing me with a second chance.

I stood on stage next to Pastor Ron Hunt, waiting for the big moment. Two friends from church began to play and sing an acoustic version of Iron and Wine's "Fever Dream" for the processional of bridesmaids and groomsmen. My eyes were fixed on the door way, waiting for my bride-to-be to enter.

Our friends began to sing "Love and Some Verses," also by Iron and Wine, in perfect harmony, like songbirds.

Everyone stood as Crissi made her entrance. She was glowing. It took every bit of willpower to fight back the tears of joy. She seemed to glide down the aisle, looking radiant in her sleeveless gown with her hair just right. I whispered to our pastor, "Doesn't she look stunning? God has blessed us, indeed." He smiled. "Yes, she does. And yes, He has!"

We honeymooned in Costa Rica, which was a dream come true for me. We each had a couple of "must-do's." I wanted to zip line and see the rainforest, and she really wanted to chill on the beach and go horseback riding. In the morning after a Costa Rican breakfast of plantains, black beans and eggs we walked along the soft beach to the tide pools. As our feet sunk into the downy sand, we saw hundreds of hermit crabs scurrying sideways beneath the mangroves in search of their breakfast. The tide pools were teaming with all kinds of colorful and interesting creatures. We were mesmerized.

On the third day we made our way up to the Arenal Volcano one of Costa Rica's several active volcanoes. After stopping at a local coffee stand for a fresh cup of Costa Rican coffee that tasted divine, we made our way up the windy road and found Tabacon resort. It is a luxurious resort that sits adjacent to Arenal, with acres of tropical grounds and streams heated from the volcano. We soaked it all in and then took a cat nap in one of the private cabanas. Once again, we felt like royalty.

On the recommendation of the hotel concierge, we took a tour of one of the rivers in Tamarindo. It was a private tour with just the two of us and our smiling tour guide, Victor. "Hear that clap? That's clams," he said in broken English and demonstrated clapping his hands together. We slowly motored up the river waters, passing locals walking along the muddy shores beneath the mangroves, digging for clams.

As we continued upstream, Victor pointed to three fresh water crocodiles snoozing in the hot sun on a muddy eddy, while a fourth swam toward us. Our guide was not worried about it, neither were the clam diggers just downstream. It was pretty cool to be that close to a wild croc, but I kept a watchful eye on it until we were further upstream.

As we meandered along the mangroves, Victor pointed out two-hundred-year-old trees covered with twelve-inch long thorns and native birds and other native wildlife and plants. He then docked the boat along "Monkey Island." We climbed off the boat and wandered through the small forest. Howler monkeys hollered at us from canopy above. One even tried to pee on me, but missed.

Our evenings were spent enjoying wonderful fresh seafood and local savory dishes, and just relaxing. Crissi wrote and read, and I watched the Giants-Cardinals playoffs. In the first few days, we made sure to post a few photos on Facebook, but kept it to a minimum the rest of the trip. We were living the dream—it was a perfect honeymoon.

The last day we were able to horseback ride up a trail to zip lines on property owned by a local family. It was a perfect honey moon. We did everything we wanted, and then some.

A week later, we returned and went back to work. I had left the newspaper the year before the wedding and took a short–term gig. I was not happy there, and, on a complete leap of faith, left without another secure job lined up yet. Two weeks later, in December, I was hired as a National Sales Manager for a local manufacturer that was only five minutes from my home. It was an incredible opportunity to learn everything I could about a line of safety products for the elderly—from manufacturing to marketing and distribution. It enabled me to travel across the country and learn as much as I could about running a business which was yet another dream fulfilled.

Crissi was pressing forward with her dreams. In March of 2013, she held her first published novel, *A Symphony of Cicadas*. Over the next few years, she would publish several more novels, including that very first manuscript, *A Road to Hope*.

My life and our relationship is very much like a road to hope. There are twists and turns and many a pothole. My story is not that different from others—we have all been tested and put through the wringer, in one way or another. Despite our past, selfish desires, faults, failures, and shortcomings, I have found that there is always a lamp at our feet to light our path, to give us a sense of purpose, and a reason to press on.

But sometimes I need to find the willingness to want to change. That desire is personal and it must come from within each individual. Nobody can or will make us change. All I know is that when I have faith, trust, and do my best in God's eyes, that is enough. He loves me, no matter what.

A few years into our marriage, I got into a big fight with my wife and was very unloving. I left the house, slamming the door behind me. I jumped into my car, raced the engine and sped off across town. For the first time in a long while, the thought of drinking sounded like a good idea. Feelings suck—especially anger and resentment. They can be so destructive. I don't even remember what Crissi and I were fighting about, probably something about parenting styles. As I sped across town, I toyed with the thought of getting beer and heading to the coast. *I'll show her!* I thought. *How stupid. I'll end up dead.*

Instead, I pulled over, opened the glove box and pulled out an AA meeting schedule. There was a meeting across town that had started fifteen minutes earlier. Better late than never.

I walked in and found a seat. I took a deep breath and listened. The topic was love. *Ha! Gotta love God's prompting and sense of humor,* I thought. In all the meetings I've been to over the years, I don't ever recall a topic of love. The topic for this meeting was all about love—loving ourselves and loving others. I sat and listened to the others share their experience, my anger dissipated and I began to feel love. The group loved me when I wasn't feeling loving toward my wife or myself, or the world around me. The meeting ended, and I left feeling as if my cup had been filled. I later apologized to my wife for my outburst.

Once again, I was reminded that nothing, absolutely nothing happens, in this world by mistake.

Miracles and Milkshakes

Whether you believe there are no mistakes or not, I do. I have seen things happen so many times that seemed wrong or painful or didn't make any sense. When I looked within, prayed, or talked it out with another, I learned to walk through whatever it was that was causing me agony inside. I came through. I survived. The key for me, is to learn to seek out the wisdom and counsel of others and a power greater than myself BEFORE I explode.... It's a work in progress. I don't know if any of you ever experience those times where you wish you would've paused when agitated. Rather than being left with the regret for doing or saying something that hurt another and, ultimately myself, I have found when I pause first, and remember to breathe, my anger dissipates.

Miracles happen every day. So do tragedies, I wish I could say the story ends here and we all lived happily ever after...that's only in movies and fairy tales.

Crissi and I were on our way to our getaway spot in the hills to unwind for the weekend. As we got to the bottom of the hill in Calistoga, the road was blocked. We found a local deli where we ordered up sandwiches. It seemed to take forever. I was famished. As my blood sugar crashed, I kept thinking, be calm, don't blow a gasket.

While we were waiting for our food, I recognized a thin man with great smile and moustache that I hadn't seen in over twenty years. It was TJ, my therapist. I had been racking my brain trying to find the name of the therapy we did that was so critical in breaking through my deep seated anger about my abandonment issues. Once again, there are no mistakes, I thought.

We exchanged simple small talk. He introduced me to his new wife. I did the same.

"He's a standup guy," he said, looking to my wife while patting me on the shoulder.

I gave him a quick update of the last twenty years, and told him about the book I was writing.

"Remember when I did that deep work, getting below the surface of all that anger around my dad? You know with the tennis racket and the cube? What was that called?"

Looking up, he searched his memory, "Biokinetics," he said.

"That was very deep and powerful work. I can't thank you enough for helping me."

"You bet. It looks like you're doing well. Keep it up!" he said with a big smile.

"So good to see you," I said giving him a hug. "Nice to meet you as well," I said to his wife.

Our food was ready. We inhaled it while looking for an alternate route to our getaway.

We needed this getaway to unwind. We were not going to turn back. We found another way through the Napa hills and Angwin, which turned out to be a beautiful drive. We arrived only an hour and a half later than we had expected, and had a great relaxing weekend.

Life is a trip. When we are fully present we start to notice things that have been there all along.

The chance meeting with my therapist and having time to "unplug" reminded me of a phone call I got from my mom in October of 2005.

"Your aunt called and said that your dad is very sick. You should go see him," she urged. "He's at Santa Rosa Memorial Hospital."

Shit. Here we go again. Another hospital visit. Why me? Why now?

"Okay. I'll stop by after work."

My heart pounded as I parked the car.

Is it too late? What if he's going to die? How am I going to handle this?

Suffocating from the 'what ifs,' I said a short prayer.

"God, please grant me the strength and courage to face this situation. To accept it for whatever it is. To come from a place of compassion and let my dad know how much I love him."

I walked into the hospital and asked the receptionist which room he was in.

She gave me the number and pointed to the room. I walked down the dimly lit hall. It was quiet. The room was dark. My dad lay in a hospital gown. He'd lost forty to fifty pounds since I last saw him three years earlier. Salt and pepper stubble covered his gaunt face. He looked very frail.

Our eyes met. His warm smile melted away all the pain and hurt and anger of the past thirty-five years.

My heart glowed with his beaming smile. He was truly delighted to see me. In that moment he showed me what it was like to let go of the past. In that moment, despite his body giving up, he was radiant.

His smile filled my heart with so much joy. I was so, so glad it wasn't too late. I really don't know how I could've handled it if I was too late.

"Hi Dad!"

"Shawn," he chuckled, "you look good!"

"Thanks Dad," I said, giving him a hug. "So what's going on?" I asked, trying to be strong.

"Some infection...they don't know."

"Wow. You've lost a lot of weight," I remarked, feeling a little uneasy and very concerned about his health. His smile didn't match his body. But he was at peace—I could see it in his warm brown eyes. He's letting go, I thought.

The stubble on his face reminded me of all the times he'd given me a hug and a kiss goodnight as a kid. I felt safe. I looked up to my dad so much as a young child. I could brag that my dad was a fireman! When he left us, all that changed. The love I felt was replaced by anger and hurt. He had abandoned me and my two brothers, and I let it imprison me. I drank over it so I wouldn't have to face the feelings. But now, the love we shared for so many years was stronger than ever. It enabled me to push through the layers of resentment, like a seedling reaching for the sunlight in spring.

As I held his hand, I felt all that love come rushing back. Fond childhood memories rushed forward. After baths as a child, he would dry my hair by vigorously rubbing it with a towel. I loved that. Now, as we talked about life and how much I loved him, once again, I asked for his forgiveness for all the anger I had held from the past.

Without thinking about it, I began to rub his head—a comforting gesture he had done for me so many times as a kid.

"Dad, I love you."

"Ha!" he chuckled. His eyes expressed peace, love and care. "I love you, too, Shawn. I'm sorry we lost Seth." His voice trailed off a bit. (We hadn't really talked about the loss of my brother since the time several years earlier. I had made amends with this as part of my recovery.) Still, his words touched a piece of the wound that still existed.

"Please let Kelly know I love him, too," he continued. "Even though I never got to see you boys much, I thought about you often. You were always with me," he said, holding his hand close to his heart, smiling. Tears streamed down my face. "I know, Dad. I know. It wasn't easy, but we all turned out all right."

"Yeah, I'm proud of you, Shawn."

I wiped the tears from my face. "Thank you. I love you, Dad. Is there anything you'd like?"

"A milkshake," he replied quickly with a childlike smile.

"A milkshake?"

"Yeah—chocolate."

I smiled at the simplicity of the request.

"I'll get you a milkshake the next time I come back, okay?"

"I'd like that." We hugged and said our goodbyes.

That was the last time I saw my father. He passed shortly thereafter.

I'm ashamed to say that I didn't make it back to get him his chocolate milkshake. I feel a little guilty. I could've just gotten it that day. I guess I'll just have to wait until I see him again. Now, every time I have a milkshake, I think of my father. I imagine us sitting on a park bench watching the ducks, sipping on a milkshake together. Somehow, that helps assuage my guilt. I feel blessed that I got to say goodbye. This experience also serves as a reminder to make peace with those closest to us—to cherish the time that we do have. Our life on this planet is so very brief. Depending on your beliefs, there's plenty of time for milkshakes in Heaven.

Chapter 26
Joy

When the drumbeat of the past subsides, and the noise in my head dissipates long enough to be still I'm able to reflect—to get lost in moments of joy....

The pure joy on Crissi's face as she walked down the aisle. And the joy on her face when she held her first novel in her hands.

The joy I felt as I listened to a video of my stepdaughter, Summer singing the song, *Oceans*, by Hillsong United in youth ministry worship while I was on the road.

The joy of our good family friend, Joannie, who hugged me to tears the first Christmas after I got sober.

The joy I felt as a kid when I watched the men of the San Geronimo Valley build the best playground ever, with massive swings, rope nets, slides, and an obstacle course—built so well, it still stands today, forty years later.

The joy of sixty childhood friends from the San Geronimo Valley, who came together, to pray, each in their own way, for the brother of a dear friend to be free of a life threatening disease. To later hear the prayer answered as that young man went on to have a family of his own.

Some joy is found in moments: sitting on a park bench and witnessing the tear in an old woman's eye as she reads the handmade birthday card from her four-year-old grandchild. Or catching the wry, flirty smile from the old farmer when the young waitress asks, "Would you like a warm up...for your coffee?" knowing full well that the harmless flirting is part of the dance that will give her the tips she needs to survive.

Recently I drove by some of the ball fields where Andrew and Lucas played baseball. I was reminded of how much joy it brought me to watch them both play.

Watching Lucas strike out the side and walk confidently off the mound after warming the bench most of the season.

Seeing Andrew race down the first base line to beat the throw for a base hit, then steal second, and moments later, score the go ahead run on a passed ball.

I loved watching these boys play baseball. Now that they've both grown up and moved on to different sports and interests, I miss sitting in those bleachers.

Several years ago, I got to manage Andrew's baseball team for one game. I had been a base coach, but the manager had been suspended for a game for contesting balls and strikes, so I had to step in and manage the team for this one game. It was the bottom of the sixth inning and we were getting our butts whooped, losing 9-0. If the other team scored one more run we'd lose by the ten-run rule.

The kids piled into the dugout between innings, and sat on the bench with their heads hung low. I decided to give the kids a little pep talk.

"Hey guys guess what? We're losing, again. Kinda sucks doesn't it?"

"Yeah."

"These guys are good, but I think you are better. Has anyone ever wondered what it would be like to come from way behind to win? You know, like the Giants when Kuiper makes the call, 'It's the bottom of the ninth, the bases are loaded...Bonds steps into the batter's box...here's the pitch...he's hit it high...he's hit it deep...that ball is OUTTA HERE!' Here's what we need to do to win—we need ten runs. We can't hit a ten run homer. Instead, I need every one of you to step into that batter's box. There's thirteen of you on this team, each of you needs to get an at bat. Ten of you need to find a way to get on base and cross home plate. You can do it. I know you can. Every one of you." Pointing to the kids, "You...and you...and you. Think you can you do that?" I asked one kid.

"Yeah," one kid spoke up.

"And you?"

"Yeah."

"And you?"

"Yeah."

And all the way down the line.

"Let's do this!"

"Yeah!" they all shouted, high-fiving each other.

"Batter up!" the ump yelled.

Over the next fifteen minutes, every single kid on the team stepped up to the plate. Most found a way to get on base—a walk, then a steal; a hit; a passed ball; a double. One by one, they began to cross the plate. Each run that scored was like a shot of hope. They were pumped—they started believing they could do it. Runs six, seven, and eight crossed the plate. They were living out the come from behind scene millions of kids have fantasized about over the years. They had come all the way back from 9-0. It came down to the final out. The score was 9-8. The crowd from both sides cheered loudly, exhorting the kids to pull off a miraculous comeback. Then, as if on cue, one of our players smashed a double against the fence to drive in two runs. As the winning run crossed the plate, the players ran out of the dugout and swarmed their teammates as if they had just won the World Series. That day, for one brief moment, they had.

We all have a purpose. We all matter. But sometimes we get so caught up in our own plans and designs that we forget to pause to look at the sunset—to watch in awe as a hawk swoops down to snatch a snake from the tall grassy field, or to let our minds drift as we watch the glowing sun set over the dark horizon.

Every one of us was put here for a reason. Some of us have known what that is for a time. Others are still searching. Still others had big dreams halted as circumstances put the brakes on. It could be something we did or what someone did to us that caused a rift. Maybe it was a divorce, a broken trust, or something even worse. We are left with anger and resentment. It blocks us from the sunlight of the spirit.

It's been said that resentments are like giving someone free rent in your head. Sadly, the person or institution we are resentful at probably has no idea why we are holding a grudge. One thing is certain—forgiveness is an eraser. When we forgive others and ourselves, the power of anger evaporates. When we forgive, we make room for a hundred forms of joy:

Being accepted to college. Graduating from college. Meeting the love of your life. Having your first child. Getting married. Or watching a two-year-old scrunch his face the time they taste lemonade.

Whatever they are, we've all had moments of bliss, where all else in the world slips away and we are fully present in mind, heart, soul and spirit.

Who knows what it is. But I encourage you to look for moments in life that put a smile on your face. Seek out the moments of love shared. Experience joy.

In most cases, I find that those moments are when I am *not* thinking about myself. Instead, I am listening, watching, and experiencing something. I am living in the light.

My son is a compassionate soul. In the summer of 2013, we had another great conversation on the way to the beach. It was a gorgeous day in September. My son had just turned eighteen.

"Wanna go to the beach?" he asked. "The waves are supposed to be six to ten feet."

"Yeah, that'd be nice."

We gathered our beach stuff—towels, boogie boards, and Smash Ball.

I made a turkey sandwich, grabbed what was left of the Doritos, and a bottle of sparkling water, and tossed them in my backpack. He grabbed a red bell pepper, an orange and made a PB&J sandwich and put them in containers, which he placed in his backpack.

We then loaded the trunk, climbed into his car and headed to Stinson.

As we crossed town and headed up D Street, I admired the Victorians that lined both sides of the road. I thought about how, just a few years earlier, he was practicing driving on this side of town. As I gazed out the window at some of the newer homes and open space along the back roads, he plugged in his iPod and played some classical music.

"So, what can you tell me about Uncle Seth?" he asked out of the blue.

I looked at him and pondered the question. I told him about Seth's wit, guts, and charm, and a few of his crazy antics.

"What else?" Andrew asked. I realized I had already told him several of the stories about Seth, but I hadn't really talked about his turmoil or how I felt after he died.

"Seth was a great brother. He loved deeply and had an incredible sense of humor," I started. "But he was fighting a lot of inner demons with drugs and alcohol that eventually won out."

Andrew nodded.

I realized that he wanted to hear more. I felt a little choked up as I thought back to the day I got the call from Dave. I looked over at Andrew as he navigated the windy turns on the way to Stinson and just blurted out, "There's a part of me that feels like he was done. He gave up. I don't know if he let go of the wheel and let the car crash or not. But my mom had told me that a few weeks before Seth crashed he had told her that if he ever gets to that dark place again he's not coming back. That stung. I knew he was struggling and did what I could to help. But ultimately, he had to find help himself. She had also said that she cried out asking God to take him one day. To take his pain away…who knows exactly what happened. All I know is I loved him and miss him dearly. Sometimes I feel his presence."

As Andrew and I pulled up to Stinson Surf and Kayak, Andrew filled out a brief questionnaire and rented me a wetsuit. The water at Stinson is cold—fifty-four to sixty-two degrees. It's far too cold to be in for very long without protection. We left the rental shop then made our way to the beach.

The waves were only three to four feet—not big, but strong enough to knock us down as we made our way out through the first line of breakers.

We floated, waiting for a big one. That was half the fun—floating, just being.

My wetsuit filled with the icy waters of the Northern California Pacific Ocean. I could taste the salty sea as I rolled over the top of a small wave, making our way toward the larger break thirty yards out.

"There's the one!" I exclaimed. "Let's get it!"

With a look that said, *I can see that it's a good wave, I don't need you to tell me about it*, he smirked We both paddled into position. Then we turned, facing the beach to line ourselves up at the base of the quickly forming wave. We kicked and paddled like crazy. I felt the wave lift me as it began to crest. I glanced over at my son and smiled.

"Yeah!" I shouted as the six to seven foot wave crested, launching us in front of the white water as it came crashing down. I cut to the left, Andrew to the right. We pressed into the wave with our boogie boards, and shifted our weight back and forth to get the most out of the short ride.

"That was awesome!" he said.

"Yeah!" We high fived.

"Let's do it again."

Though the waves are not usually very large at Stinson, I always marvel and find it exhilarating to feel the power of surf as the waves lift you and catapult you forward.

Trips to the beach and father-son ski trips are a few of those bonding moments that create memories that last a lifetime.

I will forever be grateful for the good times I got to share with my own father and grandfather; they will forever be etched in my memory.

Before his passing in April of 1995, Grandpa Langwell shared a few words of advice with me. He and my grandmother had a long happy marriage, but like any couple, they had their moments of bickering. He had a simple way to get along. Whenever my grandma would ask him to run an errand or to fix something or take out the trash or whatever her request, his response was the same—"Yes, dear."

"Precious, can you run to the store to get some milk?" she'd ask.

"Yes, dear," he'd respond with a cheerful smile, even if he didn't want to go.

Leaning from his blue recliner as he picked at an open sore on his foot that just wouldn't seem to heal, he offered another pearl of wisdom—"Never plant your roots too deep." He went on to clarify, "I mean don't get stuck in the same place." Twenty-five years hence, I now understand what he meant—don't get complacent or too comfortable; enjoy life, it's too short to squander; stay curious and never stop learning.

It's sometimes painful to reflect back on the mistakes I made—my selfish, self-centered attitude, and my need to be right rather than diplomatic. "My way or the highway," was my attitude.

My whole life I had sworn that I would not be like my dad—when I married, I would not divorce. When and if I had children, I would always be there to love and support them. Life is messy. Our sock drawer is not always organized. Sometimes we walk out the door wearing two different color shoes. It's okay. Before we can walk, we learn to crawl.

Some of us, like my son, were sprint crawlers as toddlers, but we can only get so far in life crawling. Eventually, we realize it may be better to stand. So we scoot on all fours to the edge of the coffee table and pull ourselves up. Once we feel ready, we find the courage to let go. With shaky legs we take our first step. We may temporarily lose our balance, but the table is there if we need it. This is where parents or grandparents usually come in. With wide arms and encouraging words, they cheer us on with silly faces. We wobble and fall. They help us up, and we do it again, and again, and again, until after many trials and lots of practice, we learn to walk.

Letting go. Love. Forgiveness. Transformation. Each of these, like learning to walk, require courage. It takes a willingness to be vulnerable—to ask for help and do the work necessary from the inside out to chip away at the walls we may have built to protect us.

In November of 2015, Crissi and I had been part of a leadership program in our church. At the graduation ceremony our friend and team member, Curtis Newsom, told a poignant story about letting go. He had a dream that he was a wagon driver:

Letting Go
by Curtis Newsom

On the prairie, rolling along and bouncing about, there was a man in the seat next to him,

"You know much about driving a wagon?" the man asked.

"Nah, I got this," Curtis said.

"How about horses? You know anything about them?" the man persisted.

"Nah. I got this." Curtis repeated.

The horses picked up speed to a full trot. Bouncing up and down, out of control down a windy road, and around a bend, then heading down.

The man in the seat next to him asked again, "So what are you going to do about that steep ravine up there?"

Curtis looked over and realized that the man was Jesus.

He let go of the reins.

Jesus said, "I got this."

It takes compassion to listen to someone we may not agree with. It takes faith and trust to believe that letting go and learning to love and forgive is safe. This is not just my experience, there are millions of people worldwide who have recovered from drugs and alcohol, and many other addictions, through the power of forgiveness. I can speak from personal experience—it is worth it. The rewards are amazing. Relationships are restored and we learn to love again. We get a bounce in our step and are generally more happy when we forgive.

Soul Searching

In some respects, I wish that there was no trauma in my own past. There is.

I've heard it said that all events which have hurt us leave a hole in our hearts; an emptiness. The holes never fully seem to heal. We may turn to a hundred different things in a vain attempt to take away that agony—to not feel the pain. I'm sure all of us have a measure of regret, or pain from our own past, or know someone who lived through hellish situations. How do we cope? What do we do when our heart is broken or we've lost someone close? At the risk of sounding preachy, I feel compelled to dig a little deeper into this concept of facing our demons—our own Goliaths.

There is great joy in the world, yet, there is much heartache and unresolved pain, as well.

For some, the holes make us stronger. We learn to adapt. We learn to forgive ourselves. We learn that bad things can and do happen to good people. For some, like me, we learn to rely on a higher power to carry us through. We surrender and look to a God of our understanding—pick one or none—I believe that of our own human power we are too feeble to overcome any of the deep scars on our own volition. We need something more.

Grace comes from above. Willingness comes from within. If we are willing to grow, stretch, and have the courage to face our fears and painful past and then seek help—either from trusted friends, professionals, or community based support groups, we can change. We can, ultimately, break the chains that bind us. We can drop the rock of old attitudes, beliefs, pains, and hurt. We can, in a word, forgive. This sounds simple in black and white. It is far from it. For many it may never happen. For others it may take a lifetime. It has been my experience, that, in order to break free from the pain of my past, forgiveness is requisite. We need to first forgive ourselves, then others. In so doing, we unlock the shackles that enslave us. One by one we can slowly begin the process of change.

Transformation starts with recognition of what we want to change—something has to be off, or not right for us before we even consider wanting to change. It can be a problem, a habit, behavior, or actions.

Most of that change is mental—thoughts, attitudes, beliefs, values, perceptions, etc. The other part, is action and complete surrender.

Faith, willingness, and courage to change are next. Then comes introspection, soul searching, and honest assessment of ourselves.

Finally, we embark to keep our own houses in order and apologize when we are wrong, mindful of how our attitudes and actions affect those around us. We practice kindness, patience, tolerance, love, and understanding.

When we make a conscious decision to take personal responsibility and intentionally practice adding value to the lives of others, our entire world changes. Eventually, those holes that look like pock marks on our soul become the greatest source for helping others. As we practice living a different way of life, we begin to look up again. No longer staring at our shoes, we can see the light in others. We become less concerned with selfish things and more interested in those around us—those we love.

Love is really all every one of us wants and needs. That's all a child really needs—to know they are loved. That's all a wife needs—to know she is loved and honored and respected by her husband. That's all a husband needs—to be loved and validated. Sure, we all need a little more than that. Our souls cry out for one thing and one thing only—love.

Ultimately, our past becomes a springboard to catapult us into a life filled with joy, meaning and purpose.

On a warm fall day in 1999, with cumulus clouds high overhead, my five-year-old son was kicking the soccer ball in the backyard. My mom, who had watched him on Tuesdays and Thursdays for the past few years, sat reading a book.

"Grandma! Grandma! Come here!"

"What is it, Andrew?" she asked.

With wide innocent blue eyes and a big grin he pointed to the clouds.

"Look Grandma, there's Uncle Seth. He's watching me play soccer."

Chapter 27
Let it Be

In June of 2015, all five of us—Crissi, Andrew, Summer, Lucas and I finally got to take the family vacation to Hawaii we'd waited two years for.

As we approached cruising altitude on our way to Hawaii, the Beatles "Let it Be" played from my iPhone. I was reminded of my father.

I felt deprived because my dad left us. But as I revisited the dusty memories of my youth, I realized how much my father loved me. Even though I resented him for so many years, I still loved him deeply. I miss him so much. I miss his laugh, his homemade chicken enchiladas, his rubbing my head vigorously with a towel after a bath. I miss his paintings at Christmas.

He found Heaven, I am sure. He had "made his peace." I now understand what he meant. If we are to be at peace we have to let go.

I didn't understand it then, I wasn't ready to. But our dear family friend Marty, was right that day at my brother's funeral when I told him how mad I was that my dad wasn't there. He had said, "Perhaps that's the way it's supposed to be."

I had to make my peace.

It's been said that life is like peeling back the layers of an onion—more is revealed.

As I looked out the window and into the clouds listening to the lyrics, I had a picture of my father's face smiling at me.

I was overcome with emotion.

I forgive you, Dad.

"I love you, Son."

I love you, Dad.

"What's wrong?" my wife asked, concerned at the tears streaming down my face.

"I was just listening to 'Let it Be' and had this overwhelming sense of my dad near me. I felt like I could see his spirit." Her compassionate eyes offered comfort. "I was looking out at the sky," I continued "and in an instant, I finally let go. I truly forgave him for all the hurt I felt. He told me he loved me…"

I sobbed, holding back as best I could being on a plane with 200 others. She held my hand as I cried. Each of our paths is unique. However, I now believe we are all held together by the thread of a spirit inside our souls that wants the best for us—that wants us to love and be loved, to give and to receive, to make peace with our past, and to "let go and let God." When we do, our entire perspective of life changes. We become free to experience the change of heart that leads to a full and joyous life that ultimately allows us to love ourselves.

Love, true love. In the end, that's what it's all about—a change of heart through grace, recovery, faith, hope, compassion, love, and forgiveness. Don't quit before the miracle.

The end.

Acknowledgements

Recovery cannot be done alone. In fact, it requires the help of others and a belief in a power greater than ourselves, who I call God. Thank you, God.

I am eternally grateful for the love, support, and encouragement of my recovery family. My life would not be what it is without you all.

I am overwhelmed with gratitude as I give thanks to all the people who have loved me, and who have encouraged me despite my own efforts to sabotage any modicum of success:

To all my valley friends and family—growing up in the San Geronimo Valley taught me valuable lessons about the importance of community and friendship. I love you.

A special thanks to three men who paved the way to recovery before me: Andrew, David and Marty. The story of your success planted a small seed of faith that I, too, could recover, when I was ready.

To my mother, Joan O'Connor—for your unconditional love as I hit bottom, and the notes and poems you shared that encouraged me along this incredible journey.

To my stepfather, David O' Connor—you helped me believe in myself when I lacked the confidence to push forward in all areas of my life.

To my father, Jim Langwell—you gave me a sense of wonder about faith that ultimately, led me to seek help. I love you. Your smile is forever etched on my heart and soul. One day we will share that milkshake.

To my sponsor, thank you! It's been a great ride.

To our pastoral team at New Life Christian Fellowship and my circle of mentors—thank you for continuing to push me to spiritual maturity.

For my brothers, Kelly and Seth—thank you for the moments of joy we've shared.

For my son Andrew and stepchildren, Summer and Lucas—I am so proud of the young adults you are becoming. Each of you give purpose, meaning, and joy to my life.

A special thank you to Antony Giacomini—you have no idea how many times your comments and words of encouragement gave me a second wind I needed to finish this book—I've fallen, gotten back up again more times than I can count. You are a true friend who has always been there. Thank you!

Lastly, to my wife, Crissi Langwell—you paved the way three and a half years ago to show me that writing a book is possible. What I didn't realize is how incredibly difficult it is. I cannot thank you enough for your love, support, and encouragement to get it done. You made it easier for me to believe in myself, and you cleaned up my mess and made the book publishable as my editor, cover designer, web designer and consultant. I love you bigger than the sky!

About the Author

Shawn Langwell is an advertising salesman for the Bay Area News Group. He lives in Northern California with his wife, three kids, and shadow-chasing dog, Jasper.

Shawn has over thirty years of continuous sobriety and has dedicated his life to helping others. *Beyond Recovery* is his first book.

Visit his website at www.shawnlangwell.com.

Made in the USA
Middletown, DE
29 July 2023

35902134R00179